Young Mark Twain and the Mississippi

By Harnett T. Kane

RANDOM HOUSE • NEW YORK

The author and publisher are grateful to Mr. Frederick Anderson, Editor, The Mark Twain Papers, University of California Library, Berkeley, California, for his helpful comments on the text.

Grateful acknowledgment is also due to Harper & Row, Publishers, for permission to use quotations from the following books: *The Innocents Abroad* and *Life on the Mississippi* by Mark Twain; *The Autobiography of Mark Twain*, edited by Charles Neider; *Mark Twain, A Biography* and *A Short Life of Mark Twain* by Albert Bigelow Paine; and *Mark Twain's Speeches*, edited by Albert Bigelow Paine. The first quotation on page 1 is from *Life on the Mississippi;* the second is from *The Ordeal of Mark Twain* by Van Wyck Brooks (copyright 1920, 1933 by E. P. Dutton & Co., Inc.) by permission of the publisher.

Library of Congress Cataloging-in-Publication Data:
Kane, Harnett Thomas. Young Mark Twain and the Mississippi. SUMMARY: Recounts the early life of Samuel Clemens, from his happy-go-lucky boyhood to the realization of his ambition to become a Mississippi River pilot.
   1. Twain, Mark, 1835–1910—Biography—Youth—Juvenile literature. 2. Authors, American—19th century—Biography—Juvenile literature. 3. Humorists, American—19th century—Biography—Juvenile literature.   4. Pilots and pilotage—Mississippi River Region—Biography—Juvenile literature.   5. River life—Mississippi River—Juvenile literature. 6. Mississippi River—Juvenile literature. [1. Twain, Mark, 1835–1910. 2. Authors, American] I. Title. PS1332.K36 1987   818'.409 [B] [92] 87-4531 ISBN: 0-394-89182-1 (trade); 0-394-90413-3 (lib. bdg.)

Manufactured in the United States of America   1 2 3 4 5 6 7 8 9 0

Contents

AUTHOR'S NOTE   *vi*

1. *Steamboat at the Riverbank*   3
2. *Judge Clemens of Hannibal*   11
3. *Summer in the Country*   18
4. *"A Cat in Disguise"*   31
5. *School or the River?*   39
6. *Epidemic*   47
7. *A Real Steamboat Ride*   59
8. *Boys on the Prowl*   69
9. *Turning Point*   79
10. *Printer's Devil*   88
11. *Wanderer*   102
12. *Cub Pilot*   112
13. *Reading the Water*   122
14. *Tragedy on the River*   135
15. *Mississippi Pilot*   146

Author's Note

Many of the incidents in this book are based on Samuel Clemens's recollection of his boyhood in Hannibal and his early years on the Mississippi. Now and then his memory was known to trick him on small details, but most of his descriptions are supported by later inquiry.

And in the broad sense, this is a true story—of a boy and a river and a uniquely picturesque era in American history.

HARNETT T. KANE

Young Mark Twain and the Mississippi

" . . . the great Mississippi, the majestic, the magnificent Mississippi, rolling its mile-wide tide along, shining in the sun."

"I'd rather be a pilot than anything else I've done in my life."

—SAMUEL LANGHORNE CLEMENS
(Mark Twain)

1

Steamboat at the Riverbank

"Ste-a-m-m-boat comin'!"

An old man, famous in the town for his sharp eyes and powerful voice, called out the words. He had spied a tiny smudge of dark smoke in the distance as a white vessel rounded a point of land.

Suddenly the sleeping village of Hannibal, Missouri, woke up. As the cry rang along the streets this spring morning, every boy in town stopped what he was doing. Games and chores were forgotten, and in a moment they were racing for the river landing. Among them was young Sam Clemens. Although he was not quite eight years old and smaller than the rest, he usually got there first.

Leaving tracks in the dust, Sam passed a line of Water Street shops. Their clerks had been dozing in chairs tilted against the wall. Now they yawned and rose, while other townsmen thrust their heads out of windows. Several ladies put on their bonnets and began to walk toward the river.

Around the corner rolled a cart, then another, a large dray, and a few wagons. Dogs stretched and ambled in the direction of the landing. At the edge of a wooden sidewalk, a mother pig and her young ones had been slowly sniffing along. Now even they looked interested.

Reaching the stone-paved wharf, Sam saw a familiar sleeping figure. It was Mr. Blankenship, the town loafer. The red-faced, whiskery fellow scratched and forced himself up.

As carts clattered by, turning and backing into place, Sam looked eagerly around. The waterfront was an exciting place, full of all kinds of exotic people. There were sun-browned, hard-muscled, loud-talking men who floated down the river in flatboats. There were shifty-looking gamblers, ready in a moment to fight with fists or knives or anything else that came to hand. And there were plain drifters, on the lookout for any way to acquire some ready cash. It was no wonder mothers warned their boys away from the wharf and considered it a "rough" spot.

Sam scanned the horizon. Like every youth in the river town, he could identify each of the many types of vessels—broadhorns, arks, keelboats, hay boats—

that went up and down the Mississippi. As he waited for the steamboat to come closer, his nostrils filled with the fresh, slightly muddy odor of the river.

There it spread before him—the master river of the New World, occupying the heart of a continent. In this year of 1843, the Mississippi and the many streams that flowed into it carried an enormous portion of America's trade. At Hannibal the river was a whole mile wide, almost like a sea.

To Sam, the river was a part of his life separate from any other. He loved its brooding silences, the many miles of overgrown wilderness along its quiet banks. But he also loved the excitement and adventure the Mississippi brought as the roadway to a world far beyond his town.

Sam shaded his eyes. The steamboat was coming closer, its double black smokestacks rising high above the carved wooden decks.

"It's the *Missouri*!" Sam shouted to anyone who might be listening. He could identify any steamboat in regular service at Hannibal as soon as it came into sight.

"Got the freight ready?" a man called to someone behind him.

"Everything's packed, packed tight."

Sam looked in the growing crowd for his friend, Mr. Stavely. Nobody had ever heard of a steamboat docking before the town saddler arrived. Mr. Stavely had never been known to meet a friend or receive a shipment of goods from a vessel, but he liked to look as if he expected thousands of saddles and had to be ready to receive them. Watching his flying coattails as he swept by, strangers were always much impressed and so was Sam.

The throb of the steamboat's engines was like a familiar welcome song to young Sam. He knew every line of the vessel—long and trim, spick-and-span, sparkling as if a giant carpenter had just finished cutting it out and dipping it in paint. Between the pair of black chimneys hung a heavy gilded anchor. Each steamboat had such a symbol—a cotton bale, an animal's head, an anchor—proclaiming its identity to the world.

At the side of the boat were paddle-wheel boxes decorated with handsome pictures. Here were scenes of a vivid sunset on the Mississippi or a castle on the Rhine River in Germany. Some boats had only the vessel's name with golden rays around it. To Sam and the other boys of Hannibal, such paintings were the most splendid on earth.

As always, Sam's gaze went up to the steamboat's place of command, a glass and wooden box in which the pilot stood at the steering wheel. This was the heart of the boat, the place from which orders went to the enginemen who worked below. Ornamented like the rest of the boat in "gingerbread" woodwork, the pilothouse perched upon the deck where the officers slept.

Out of the corner of his eye, Sam saw Mr. Stavely arrive breathlessly at the landing. People began to exchange cries of greeting with friends on board as the vessel rolled steadily nearer. Dozens of faces filled the space above the upper rail.

Sam's eyes dropped to the boiler deck, where the open furnace doors showed the fire dancing in the engines. To him the furnaces were like hungry monsters, never satisfied no matter how much wood the workers tossed in. Some of the ladies used dainty handkerchiefs to wave the fumes away, but Sam drank them in delightedly. He liked even the smoke smell of a steamboat.

Now the captain, a big-stomached, white-haired man, surveyed the scene like a king, ready to signal for the vessel's landing. Sam heard the steam whining through the engine valves. On the forward part of the deck, members of the crew waited to jump to their duties. Over the bow went a stage plank, soon to be lowered at the landing. And Sam's quick eyes followed every movement of a young deck hand who stood at the end of the plank, a heavy rope in his hand.

The moment arrived. The captain's plump, newly manicured hand rose, the bell clanged, and there came a sudden silence as the wheels stopped. Almost at once a boiling foam in the water sent spray over Sam and others at the landing. The deck hand threw his rope ashore, tightened it, and a new kind of confusion broke out.

Sam was shoved aside and stepped on in the bustle of passengers disembarking. Men and women with carpetbags pushed forward, their servants with larger packages behind them. Workmen bearing boxes of freight tried to get off, colliding with those who were attempting to board the boat.

A woman shrieked as she lost a handbox, and a father caught his son by the seat of his breeches in time to rescue him from a swim in the Mississippi. On the wharf, mothers threw their arms around sons returning from long trips, and wept as they held them.

Sparks fell from the stacks and one or two missed Sam by inches, but he scarcely noticed. Intently examining the passengers, he made out dignified gentlemen in stovepipe hats; ladies wearing wide, flowing skirts and big scoop bonnets. There were gaunt, unshaven workers on their way to new jobs down the river; prosperous-looking merchants with cigars poking at angles from their mouths; lean, earnest ministers and schoolteachers; burly German settlers—all of them a part of the great world that traveled the Mississippi. Sam even noticed a few women with powder and rouge on their faces—something that no lady in Hannibal would ever dare attempt.

Meanwhile the vessel's big, husky mates yelled and shook their fists at the roustabouts moving back and forth with the freight. This was pandemonium, but pandemonium on a schedule. As everybody knew, the vessel would have only ten minutes at Hannibal. Then, whether or not all newcomers had boarded, and all who planned to disembark had done so, the captain signaled for the steamboat's departure.

As Sam watched with a quick-beating heart, engines moved again and the water made a heavy foam. Slowly, like a living creature, the steamboat slipped away from the bank. The show had ended.

Some of the people of Hannibal turned away, but Sam Clemens stayed on the wharf. He saw the pale vessel grow steadily smaller until it seemed like a child's toy bobbing on the river. Smoke billowed from the double chimneys, floating behind like a graceful plume. Then finally, rounding a bend, the steamboat was gone.

The clerks of Hannibal returned to their chairs tilted against the wall. Carts rolled away, dogs trotted off, and the sow and her little pigs rambled to a side lane. Mr. Stavely went back to his saddlery. And still Sam remained on his feet at the top of the landing.

Someday, he told himself, he would ride on one of those magnificent boats. More than that, he was going to be a part of their world—the boy who threw the rope from the stage plank, or one of the mates. Or perhaps, if fortune was kind to him, he might even become a pilot. At the last thought, his heart beat more quickly. That would be the best life of all.

Starting toward home, Sam stopped beside a ditch. His quick eye had caught a flash of green movement. Squatting down, he bent forward. Yes, there it was. His hand shot out and he had it, a small, blinking frog.

He had always liked frogs, no matter how much his mother and his sister, Pamela, shuddered when they saw them. Sam grinned. He had an idea for a good use for this one. Whistling, he continued on his way.

2

Judge Clemens of Hannibal

Mrs. Jane Clemens, a small, pretty woman of forty, stood in the doorway of her narrow-fronted house. Her worried expression changed to a smile as she spied her son Sam, kicking up dust as he ambled along. She should have known he had been at the Mississippi landing.

The boy halted before Mrs. Clemens. "I have a surprise for you in my right pocket." His innocent air made it appear that this would be a real treat. Pleased, his mother reached in. She let out a scream as she brought forth the moist green frog.

"Sammy!" Mrs. Clemens shook her head. "One of those pesky things again." Delighted to be freed, the frog gave one hop, then another, and reached the street, followed with eager interest by six young, furry cats.

The Clemens household was always heavily populated by cats. At present there were fifteen, and once Sam had counted nineteen, in all shapes, colors, and breeds. The rest of the family tolerated the cats, but Sam and his mother loved them. Whenever the other Clemenses sat down, they looked around carefully, because cats seemed to be everywhere.

Mrs. Clemens turned to go inside, saying, "Don't go away, boy. Your pa's due back from his trip, and this time I feel sure he'll have good news."

At the word *trip,* the boy's heart beat a little faster. To be able to travel, for even a short distance, sounded like the finest thing in life to Sam. At least once, his father had been all the way down to Memphis, Tennessee. Mr. Clemens also spoke of Vicksburg, Natchez, and other river centers with fine-sounding names. Someday, Sam assured himself, he was going to visit every one of those towns, if it took him all his life.

But no matter how hopeful Mrs. Clemens appeared, Sam had doubts about his father's prospect of success on his present trip. Things had been going poorly for the family, worse than he could ever remember.

On both sides the Clemens family considered itself Southern, with roots back in the older, quieter states.

Mrs. Clemens insisted that one branch of her people was descended from an English earl. Sam's father told of an ancestor who had sat in the British Parliament and voted for the execution of a king who was a tyrant.

But the present-day Clemenses had come down in the world. Sam's father was "Judge" John Marshall Clemens, Hannibal's justice of the peace. It was a position of high respect but small salary. Mr. Clemens was a lawyer, but in Hannibal, which had fewer than fifteen hundred people, there appeared to be little business for lawyers. "A fine man," Sam heard people say. "Still, he isn't doing very well."

The judge had been born in Virginia in the hilly, not-so-fertile uplands. The family had a farm with a few slaves. When the boy was only seven, however, his father had gone to a country "house-raising" to help a neighbor make a new start. A log rolled on him, and he died of his injuries. John Clemens was the oldest of the five children, and upon his shoulders fell much of the burden of the family. From then on he worked long hours with little rest.

Sam Clemens was to remember his father as a serious, conscientious man. He was lean and thin-faced, and people said that his constant struggle showed in his eyes. He worked hard to pay every bill and meet even the smallest obligation.

After the family moved from Virginia to the

"western" country of Kentucky, John Clemens met a vivacious girl who liked to laugh and dance. Her name was Jane Lampton and her family had also moved west from Virginia. The couple fell in love, were married, and started out together for Tennessee with several slaves. There they bought a tract of thousands of acres of wooded land, which Mr. Clemens never gave up. "Someday that land will make us rich," he said again and again.

But the Clemenses were far from wealthy. They farmed a small part of their property, and the young husband tried law. These were times of depression, however, that lasted for years. The couple sold their slaves, one by one, for money to live on. Then they heard of new opportunities farther west, in Missouri, and struck out one day for the new area.

In Missouri the Clemens family went first to a village thirty miles from the Mississippi River. It was named Florida, and here Sam was born on November 30, 1835. He arrived on earth on a night when thousands peered into the sky at a weird glowing object with a long tail behind it—the famous Halley's Comet. Jokingly Sam boasted that this meant he was something special.

The village of Florida was so tiny that Sam later called it "almost invisible." It had a hundred people and, simply by being born, Sam increased the population by one percent. He wrote: "It is more than many of the best men in history could have done for a town. . . . There is no record of a person doing as much—not even Shakespeare."

The village had two streets, each about two hundred yards long. The rest of Florida consisted of wandering lanes surrounded by cornfields and rail fences. Roads and lanes were all paved with the same material—in Sam's words, "tough black mud in wet times, deep dust in dry." With his brother-in-law, John Quarles, Judge Clemens tried to run a store. But it failed, and in 1839 the family moved to Hannibal. From then on the Mississippi was part of the boy's life.

In Hannibal family problems grew. Several men in various places owed money to Judge Clemens, but he could not collect from them. "If only one would make good his just debts!" Jane Clemens would exclaim. "If you weren't so understanding, if you forced them to pay. . ." But Sam's father could never do that.

They had had to move to a smaller house since they had come to Hannibal and now, with their debts growing higher, they might have to make another change. A year or so earlier Sam's older brother, Orion, a dreamy, impractical youth of seventeen, had gone to St. Louis to learn to be a printer. Some claimed this was a step downward for a lawyer's son, but the Clemenses needed every dollar they could get. With the family lived Sam; his older sister, the gentle and kindly Pamela; and the youngest child, the well-behaved Henry.

Now, sitting on the back steps, Sam stroked one of the newest kittens and listened for the purring like a motor inside its chest. Was there anything as friendly or as beautiful as a cat?

A familiar figure sauntered into the yard and Sam looked up with a grin. "Tom! Tom Blankenship!"

A bit older than most of Sam's friends, Tom was tall, roughly dressed, careless in appearance. All parents disapproved of him because his father was the town loafer. But, in Sam's words, "he was the only really independent person—boy or man—in the community," and he was continually happy. While Sam could go barefoot only in summer, Tom never wore shoes at any time. It was no wonder he was admired and envied by the other boys.

Although he had no thought of writing at this time, Sam was eventually going to make Tom one of the greatest of his literary characters—Huckleberry Finn.

Delighted to see his friend this afternoon, Sam shifted to make a place beside himself. Tom rubbed his knee where his trouser leg had been torn, and yawned. "A couple of us is settin' out to go fishin'," he drawled, "and I thought you might join us."

"Gee," Sam replied happily, "I can't think of anything I'd rather do."

Suddenly a deep voice rose from the doorway. "I'm afraid you won't be able to make it today, Sam."

It was his father. Judge Clemens's lean face showed his disapproval of Tom, but he remained polite. "Some other time, my boy," he said.

Sam tried to hide his disappointment as Tom started away with a shrug. "Well, so long." Sadly Sam looked on as Tom joined another friend at the corner and headed toward the river.

Sam turned to go inside. He stopped as he heard his mother asking, "Did the trip go well, Judge?"

"No, my dear. The man won't pay, though I tried everything." The tired voice died away and Sam watched Judge Clemens's shoulders sag as he dropped into a chair. His mother's idea that things were going to improve had been wrong, and she would not joke so easily tonight.

Summer in the Country

Early one summer morning Sam climbed up on the wide seat of his uncle John's wagon. Holding tightly to a basket containing his favorite cat of the moment, he waved good-bye to the rest of the family. Uncle John clucked to the horses, and Sam was off to spend the summer at the Quarles farm near Florida, Missouri.

Sam had been sickly as a small child and, he later recalled, had existed mainly on medicines. His mother took every opportunity to send him to the country for his health. To Sam's mind, the farm was the only place that could compete with the Mississippi as a source of delight.

While the wagon was rattling down the dusty road, Sam stole a last look at his river and thought how much he would miss it. But he knew he couldn't very well be in two places at once, and his spirits rose with every mile of the journey.

Hours later the wagon creaked up a heavily wooded hill and Sam shouted as he recognized the old gray-brown farmhouse.

"Here we are!" called Uncle John, a wide grin splitting his plump face, and in a moment the rest of his family appeared.

The whole population of the Quarles farm had an easygoing air—the eight children, father, mother, and the twenty black slaves. Now most of them ran forward. "Sammy, Sammy!" cried Aunt Patsy. "Boy, you've gotten thin again. But we have just the things inside to put the pounds right back on you."

As his aunt half smothered him in her arms, Sam smiled. He looked around to see if everything was as he remembered it. Ahead rose the house, a double one built of logs with a covered wooden passage running between. Here the family could have its meals practically in the open. A short distance away the hill dropped off to the barns, stables, corncrib, and a rich-smelling building for tobacco-curing.

"Sammy, what are you doing? Come on in!" The Quarles boys and girls clustered around him, and something else urged him forward—the delectable aromas from the table. He would never, never forget the things he enjoyed here:

"Fried chicken, roast pig; wild and tame turkeys, ducks and geese; venison just killed; squirrels, rabbits, pheasants, partridges, prairie chickens; biscuits, hot batter cakes, hot buckwheat cakes, hot 'wheat bread,' hot rolls, hot corn pone; fresh corn boiled on the ear, succotash, butter beans, string beans, tomatoes, peas, Irish potatoes, sweet potatoes; buttermilk, sweet milk, 'clabber'; watermelons, muskmelons, cantaloupes—all fresh from the garden; apple pie, peach pie, pumpkin pie, apple dumplings, peach cobbler—I can't remember the rest."

And this rich, fresh menu was prepared so well! After he had gone around the world, Sam declared that nothing tasted like the fried chicken of his boyhood. Nobody—not the great plump chefs of France, or the beaming housewives of Germany, or the pink-cheeked cooks of English inns—could serve chicken like that. And no bread could match the loaves that steamed in the morning light in Aunt Patsy's kitchen.

Today so many things had been heaped about the center of the long table that the family had trouble finding space for their plates along the outside. Eventually, their stomachs bulging, they left the table and the Quarles boys and girls led Sam on his long-awaited inspection of the place.

They ran among the trees and jumped up to snatch at the branches. They patted the manes of the horses, rubbed the warm flesh of the cows, and sniffed at the tobacco plants in the field. "The smokehouse!" Sam cried, and pushed his way into the shadowy building, with its woody scent and rows of fat hams hanging in the air.

"Let's find the swings!" he urged a minute later. Although twilight would soon be upon them, they darted toward the clearing where seven swings hung from branches of the trees.

At times they soared forty feet in the air, so that the highest leaves brushed their cheeks, and the sky came so close that Sam thought his toes could touch it. Shutting his eyes, he imagined he was an eagle in the clouds.

"Uh-oh!" He heard a snap, and the swing next to his broke. The Quarles boy who had been in it tumbled to the ground and looked dazed for a moment, but got up with a smile. Sam estimated that at one time or another his cousins broke fourteen arms among the eight of them. Today, however, there were no broken bones.

"Time to go back," one of the girls murmured, and all of them ran up the hill.

That night, tired from his exertions, Sam sat contentedly on the floor of the "family room." The air had taken a slight chill, as it often did in the country, and hickory logs blazed in the enormous fireplace.

Sam watched the biggest log with care, for a sweet sap oozed out, which he and the other children would snatch off and swallow happily.

On the hearthstone Sam's cat rose, stretched himself slowly, and let the boy lift him to his lap. Gazing into the fire, Sam soon dozed off. Only half awake, he let himself be led upstairs to his room just under the sloping attic.

For a little while rain fell. How snug he felt, listening to the patter so close to his ears.

The next morning Sam rose early and, after a full breakfast, said to the other boys, "Let's find out what's happening around the place." They sped off together, with two of the girls trailing them. For some time they walked through the never-ending dusk of the woods, breathing the fragrance of dark earth mold and catching glimpses of red and purple wild flowers covered with early dew. Suddenly one of Sam's cousins whispered, "Pheasants, right over there!" They caught a flurry of movement, and then the feathered creatures were gone.

The boys ranged farther afield, seeking persimmons and pawpaws and hazelnuts. Smashing the nuts, Sam ignored the stain that the strongest soap could not remove from his clothes. "Blackberries," he called, and soon they had swept the bush clean, the dark berries leaving their own stain on lips and shirts.

Before they finished, Sam lifted his hand. "Keep still." Near his feet there was a slippery movement, a dark, gleaming shape. "Black snake!" he whispered, and his words were hardly out before the rest of them were running away. Nobody with sense fooled around with a black snake.

They followed the brook for a while, and Sam found a pretty, harmless garter snake. He held it gently, lifting it to his face and feeling the texture of its skin. One of the girls screamed, and that gave Sam another idea. He was well aware that his aunt Patsy was "prejudiced against snakes." When they trooped back to the farmhouse for the midday meal, he crept over to Aunt Patsy's workbasket and deposited the garter snake there.

After the meal, Aunt Patsy picked up her basket. Sam watched his aunt's pink fingers go reaching into it. Then, as a long object crawled out, she uttered a high scream.

Although Sam blinked innocently, Aunt Patsy turned toward him with a suspicious stare. Because it was the first day of his visit, she said nothing. The next time it happened—and of course it was certain to happen again—he would receive a brisk spanking.

After an afternoon of further explorations, one of the boys asked, "After supper, wouldn't you like to go to the quarters?"

Sam jumped in delight, for he had been wondering

when he dared ask for the privilege. The cabins behind the house held some of his favorite people. Aunt Patsy hesitated before granting permission for the trip. "Well, if you don't stay *too* long, and don't get too excited over the stories you hear," she agreed finally. Sam and the others promised, and off they went.

One of Sam's cousins suggested they first visit an elderly slave woman known as Aunt Hannah. Sam nodded; she was always good for a real chill. When they knocked at the door of her cabin, a thin voice told them: "Come in, whoever you be!"

They pushed the door open, and there in the flickering light of a fire a tiny figure sat up in bed. "Oh, it's Sammy. Come here, boy!" A tiny, withered hand—like a mummy's, Sam told himself—took hold of his.

In the uncertain light he studied the top of Aunt Hannah's head. Yes, it was still there, her round bald spot. No one had to remind him how it had gotten there. The children had heard many times from the younger slaves that she was a thousand years old and had lived in Egypt back in biblical days. People said that Hannah had been at the scene when the wicked Pharaoh drowned in the Nile, and she had been so scared that her hair fell out!

Aunt Hannah believed strongly in prayer, he understood, but when she had a very hard case to handle, she turned to witchcraft and magic. Now Sam noticed that although she had very little hair left, she had tied it up with white threads in dozens of plaits.

"What—what are they for?" Probably he shouldn't have asked, but it was impossible to keep back the question.

Aunt Hannah looked behind her into the shadows and pulled his ear close to her quivering lips. "Don't you tell anybody, boy, you hear?" Fascinated, Sam nodded, and she went on. "Somebody's tryin' to magic me. I've got a spirit workin' on me day and night, under the house, in the tree over there, everywhere."

Sam peered toward the tree that touched the window but, alas, could see nothing. Aunt Hannah finished: "Those knots in my hair keep harm away. If anybody ever try to witch you, you do the same, you understand?"

Much impressed, Sam nodded. When he had troubles again, he might try the remedy. Firmly one of his cousins took his elbow. "Uncle Daniel's next." With polite good-byes, they left Aunt Hannah.

A few yards away was the hut of "Uncle Daniel." He was middle-aged, strong-shouldered, and kindly, and the children loved him. When he talked, they listened to every word, understanding that this was a man who never told a lie, and spoke only of things he knew. Sam thought he learned more from him than from almost anyone else he met in Missouri.

"Well, now, if it isn't Sammy Clemens," Uncle Daniel greeted him. "Come in, Sammy, and every one of you." He asked a question that made Sam's heart thump with joy: "Would you like to go on a possum hunt sometime soon? . . . Yes? I kind of thought you might."

The children listened as Uncle Daniel talked about bluejays and squirrels, rabbits and hawks. He knew every creature in the woods and its habits—its good points and bad. "Tell us about the Bible," one of the boys finally urged.

"What part of the Bible?"

"Any part!" Sam replied. Uncle Daniel seemed familiar with every passage. For a half-hour or so the boy sat contentedly on the floor as Uncle Daniel told the story of David and the giant, Goliath. Then a silence fell, and Sam said something that was in the minds of all the children. "Please, Uncle Daniel, a ghost story."

"You children already heard all my stories," Uncle Daniel protested.

"That doesn't matter," Sam cried. "We still like them."

"Well, then, how about 'The Golden Arm'?"

The cry that rose from his listeners gave Uncle Daniel his answer. Although they had heard it a dozen times, they would never tire of it. In the flickering light the group sat spellbound, missing no word, no syllable.

"There was this mean old man, and he had a wife with a golden arm. . . ." Like a master storyteller, Uncle Daniel described the way the magical arm glowed in the night, and how the disagreeable husband stared at it and wondered how much money it would bring if his wife would ever give it up. But the wife treasured her peculiar arm, and he could never get it from her.

Then, Uncle Daniel continued, the wife died, and the deacons of the church buried her. Alone, the greedy husband thought of his wife in her coffin with that valuable arm. It wasn't doing anybody any good down there, was it? At last the man could no longer bear the situation; he was going to have the arm.

In the still of the night, the husband jumped over the wall of the cemetery, dug up the coffin, reached in, and pulled off his wife's arm. Home again, he gloated over his good fortune—until he heard faint footsteps from somewhere near him, and outside the window a slow rapping, rapping, rapping.

From the dark, a moan sounded. "Wh-e-re's my golden arm?" The man made no answer; perhaps his wife would go away. But the voice drew nearer: "Wh-e-re's my golden arm?" Still the husband kept silent. Before long the ghost moved up the stairs, across the landing, and then it was at his elbow, groaning and moaning: "Wh-e-re's my golden arm?" The children shuddered in anticipation. They knew what happened next, but it didn't matter.

"Wh-e-re's my golden arm?" The ghost-voice grew louder than ever, and suddenly Uncle Daniel swung around and grabbed Sam. "*You've* got it!" A wild shriek rose from the boy's lips and from those of his cousins. No matter how many times they heard the story, it was always delightfully chilling.

Later that night Sam lay in his bed listening to the whine of the wind against the roof. He heard a cracking sound. It was the old building settling a little in the night, as most old buildings do. But for a moment Sam thought it might be a spirit hunting for its golden arm. He snatched at the blanket and pulled it over his head.

The summer passed quickly, as it always did on the farm. With Uncle Daniel and several of the boys, Sam went out in the dark to hunt raccoons and possum. And there were early morning squirrel, prairie chicken, and wild-turkey hunts.

Dawn was far away when Sam and the rest of the boys got up, bad-tempered and yawning. A blast on a horn and the dogs swarmed around, panting for the chase to start. For an hour or longer the party would stumble forward. Gradually a pale light began to appear and the sky turned pink, then red, casting a glow over the damp earth.

Bang, bang! Guns fired, boys ran, Uncle Daniel shouted. Some hours later they started home, game piled over their shoulders, their appetites raging. They had traveled for miles, yet it was still only time for breakfast.

This summer, more than ever, Sam learned the delights of country watermelons—how to discover the best ones as they lay with their plump green stomachs toward the sun, how to separate them from the vines, and how to tell by thumping when they were at their peak of ripe perfection. He never forgot the sharp cracking sound as the knife sank through the dark green skin, splitting the melon into beautiful halves. Then the moist red meat with its fat black seeds lay open on the table, and the feast began. But if it was a melon that the boys had "borrowed" from the field when nobody was looking, it tasted best of all.

Even school was pleasant in the country. For one thing, it was held only once or twice a week, and the three-mile walk through the silent, echoing forest was a lively, often joyous event. In their baskets the children carried corn dodgers, buttermilk, and bits of this and that from the table. Eaten under the shade

29

of the trees at noon, everything had a rare and special flavor.

Sam had one humiliating experience when a husky girl, a few years older than he and dressed in calico and a sunbonnet, inquired if he used tobacco—that is, chewed it. When he shook his head, she gave him a look of contempt and shouted his shame to everybody: "Here's a boy that can't chew!"

The summer days flew by and soon it was time to return to Hannibal. Kisses, handshakes, waves, and shouts of good-bye accompanied Sam's departure as the wagon rolled off down the hill.

Sam dozed during the trip home. But when they approached Hannibal, he craned his neck for his first glimpse of the Mississippi. The moment they arrived, he ran toward the landing place.

"Steamboat! Steamboat comin'!"

He had come back at the finest of possible moments. There she was, plowing her way up the river, her chimneys rising bravely in the autumn light.

Sam Clemens smiled contentedly. He was home again.

"A Cat in Disguise"

People used to say that cats had nine lives. No matter what happened to them, they would come back to life again—until the ninth time. Sam Clemens claimed much the same thing about himself, and would tell the details to anyone who would listen.

Living so near the river, he seemed determined to jump in whenever he saw it. This led to a series of near disasters. Although his mother worried, she could still joke about the situation. Once, when Sam was brought in after being fished from the water, Mrs. Clemens said, "I guess there wasn't much danger. People born to be hanged are safe in water."

Sam's first experience with drowning occurred when he was playing along the banks of nearby Bear Creek. (Sam said it received its name because there were no bears anywhere along it.) He was sitting on a log, which he thought was attached to a raft. It was not, and when it tilted he rolled off.

Too frightened to shout, the boy thrashed around and sank under the surface. Rising to the top, he looked wildly about and went down a second time. He struggled to the surface again, stared at the sky, and was about to sink beneath the water for the third time when someone caught his hand. It was an old slave woman who belonged to a friend of the Clemenses.

Seizing Sam, she dragged him to the shore. He spluttered, spat out the part of the creek that he had swallowed, and finally opened his eyes. The woman had saved his life.

Did this keep Sam Clemens away from the water? It did for several days. After that he fell in once more. A youth who worked for the same neighbor happened to pass "just at the wrong time," Sam later said. The young man leaped in, felt along the bottom, and pulled him out.

"I was drowned seven times after that," Sam recalled, first in Bear Creek and then, moving to bigger and deeper things, six times in the Mississippi. In each case he was rescued just in time, and people decided that he was a cat in disguise.

Eventually his mother hit upon a scheme to protect him from the great river. To make certain he would not go into the water without her knowledge, she carefully sewed together the two sides of his shirt collar whenever he left home. If he took off his clothes to go swimming she would know at a glance because the thread would be broken.

Mrs. Clemens thought the plan was working well until Sam walked into the house one day with an unnaturally innocent air. His mother investigated and found that his collar was sewed tightly together. But Sam's younger brother, Henry, pointed out: "Ma, the thread's a different color from what you used." Investigating, she discovered that Henry was correct. She had sewed the collar in white. When Sam came out of the water, he had sewed it back in black.

Henry was a good, truthful boy, and generally Sam would agree with anybody about his brother's merits. "He never did harm to anybody, he never offended anybody," said Sam. "He was exasperatingly good."

Still, Sam was always hoping for a chance to report Henry for some misbehavior. One day he thought his opportunity had come. Sam had a habit of watching the sugar bowl. When no one was present, he would slip pieces of the old-time brown sugar from the container. Taken in that way, the sugar tasted better, Sam insisted. For him forbidden fruit always had a more interesting flavor than any other kind. By contrast Henry reached in openly for his sugar and Mrs. Clemens sensed that he would never remove any when she was not looking. With Sam she had her doubts. As he himself admitted: "Not exactly doubts, either. She knew very well I *would*."

One morning, as Henry's fingers entered the bowl, it fell and broke in pieces. It was a fine old English bowl, a family heirloom. Sam's spirits rose. It would be the first time he had ever had a chance to tell on Henry about anything.

When Mrs. Clemens walked in, she stared in horror. Before Sam could open his mouth, she hit him on the head with her thimble. He felt the blow "all the way down to my heels." Sam was now the horrified one. In an injured voice he cried, "I didn't do it, I didn't! It was Henry."

If Sam expected his mother to show regret, he was disappointed. Quietly Mrs. Clemens told him: "That doesn't matter. You deserve it—for something you're *going* to do that I won't hear about!"

Sam brooded. This wasn't fair at all. Soon afterward he had an opportunity to get revenge on Henry. Mrs. Clemens sent the smaller boy with a tin bucket to perform an errand in the back part of the house. He would have to use the outer stairway leading to the second floor. Quickly Sam locked the door from the inside so that Henry could not get in. Then he ran downstairs.

The innocent Henry started up the stairway. The garden at the side of the house had just been plowed. Seizing thick handfuls of mud, Sam pelted Henry again and again.

Henry was still on the steps, trying to block the blows with the bucket, when their mother appeared. "What are you doing?" she demanded of Sam, but he shrugged: "Oh, I'm just amusing Henry." Mrs. Clemens thought this was a very peculiar way to amuse someone, and both she and Henry started toward Sam. He escaped by jumping over a high board fence.

Several hours later Sam crept back to the yard. The coast was clear, he thought, and the whole matter had ended. The next thing he knew, a stone came sailing through the air and left a lump, "which felt like the Matterhorn," on the side of his head. The younger boy had his revenge.

Another time Sam was enjoying an afternoon in an upstairs room with half a watermelon, beautifully ripe and wonderfully red. With his knife he removed one crisp, dripping hunk after another until he had swallowed the last bit. Only the big green shell was left.

Suddenly an inspiration came to Sam. Why not

drop it on somebody's head? For a few minutes he watched as one person after another walked by. No, this man wasn't a safe object; no, that girl wouldn't do either. Now, however, precisely the right one approached—Henry.

With extreme care Sam held the watermelon shell out the window and with great cunning he began to calculate. His brother had six steps to go when Sam let the weapon drop. He later commented, "It was lovely to see those two bodies gradually closing in on each other."

If Henry had advanced seven steps, or five, the bombardment would have been a failure. But Henry took exactly the right number of steps. The shell crashed on the top of his head and "drove him into the earth up to the chin," Sam said, exaggerating as he often did.

Drawing back from the window, Sam felt the impulse to go to the street and sympathize with his brother. But he decided it would not be wise. Henry knew him so well that he might guess who the villain was.

For several days nothing more happened. Then one morning Sam sauntered by the house and caught his punishment. On *his* head Henry landed a rock that left a bump "so large that I had to wear two hats." When Sam went furiously to Mrs. Clemens to show her the terrible lump, she shrugged. He must have deserved it, she said, and he must take it as a good lesson.

Not long afterward a cholera epidemic struck the village. Sam's mother—always ready to try any remedy—pounced delightedly upon a strange, burning medicine called Pain Killer to keep her boys healthy. Sam hated the mixture because, he said, it did not kill his pain, but gave him a brand-new one.

Mrs. Clemens had two large bottles of Pain Killer, one for Sam and one for Henry. Although she could trust Henry to take his, she certainly could not trust Sam. So each morning she marked the label on Sam's bottle at a certain level, in order to tell whether or not he had swallowed his dose.

Every day Sam carefully took out his teaspoonful of the mixture, and his mother was satisfied. But she forgot that there were cracks in the floor. For days Sam fed Pain Killer to the cracks, "with very good results." The epidemic never broke out under their house, he said.

Once, as he was pouring out the medicine, one of his many cats rubbed up to him, meowing as if begging for Pain Killer. Sam told Peter the cat, "You mustn't ask for it unless you really want it." Peter kept on crying. "You'd better be sure," Sam warned. Peter made sounds that indicated he was positive he yearned for the medicine.

So Sam gave Peter a good-size dose. The cat spun into the air and went into hysterics. Swinging around the room, he bumped into chairs and tables. Then he jumped to the window, knocked down several flowerpots, and leaped out, carrying the rest of the pots with him. Peter eventually recovered, but after that only the floor cracks received Pain Killer.

School or the River?

When he had a choice between the broad, gleaming Mississippi and a crowded schoolroom with books, slates, and a firm-eyed teacher, Sam Clemens said he was somehow inclined toward the river. He struggled hard, and sometimes school—or, more accurately, fear of the teacher and his parents—won out. But not always.

One sunshiny fall day Sam started toward Mrs. Horr's school, which was conducted in an ancient, ramshackle log cabin at the end of Main Street. The birds sang energetically in the woods along the Mississippi, and Sam caught glimpses of the water, glistening like silver in the warm sunlight. What a fine day, and to think of spending it cooped up in class, with dark walls on all four sides! If he were there, he probably would be punished for something. He was *always* being punished in that place.

It had started on his very first day in school. He had broken a rule, and Mrs. Horr had told him not to do it again. When he did, the teacher informed him that he would have to be whipped. "Go out and find a switch, Sam, and fetch it in."

At least, Sam had assured himself, he could pick out his own instrument of punishment. On the ground outside the school he found several firm pieces of wood, but he passed over them. Across the way stood a cooper shop, and several thin wooden shavings had drifted toward the school building. A moment later he stood before the teacher's desk with a small shaving in his hand, looking as meek and pitiful as he could.

Mrs. Horr glanced from him to the tiny switch and back again. Then she snapped out: "Samuel Langhorne Clemens!" He had seldom heard his full name in that fashion, and by now he realized it meant real trouble. "I'm ashamed of you," Mrs. Horr said. "I'll have to call on a boy with a better judgment for switches."

Sam was depressed when he saw how many young faces brightened at the prospect of getting the assignment. The one who received it went out swiftly, returned promptly, and proved himself a true expert. The switch was an enormous object, long and thick, and for hours afterward Sam remembered its strength and its weight.

And now, going to school as slowly as possible without actually standing still, Sam thought again about the brightness of the sky and the appeal of the cool, refreshing river. Reaching class, he continued to think about it. Just before afternoon lessons began he spied John Briggs, a fellow spirit. A year or so younger than Sam, John was a big boy with bulging muscles.

Sam looked at John Briggs, and John looked at Sam.

"Wouldn't it be a fine day to go over to Glasscock's Island?" Sam asked. "We could fish and dig up turtle eggs." The words were hardly out when the other boy agreed, and they slipped away from school. When they reached the riverbank they borrowed a skiff, neglecting to tell its owner, and began to row out in a brisk breeze. "We'll be back before they miss the boat," Sam said confidently.

Their spirits improving with every moment, the boys applied themselves to the oars. The trees on the Missouri side grew smaller as they crossed the river, which was as calm as a glassy lake. Sam knew, though, that beneath the surface its strength was enormous and deadly.

Their destination was a grassy island on the Illinois side, with a sand bar extending into the water at its head. Here, with small waves lapping around them, the boys had a retreat from the world, with no parents to watch them, no teachers to correct them, no fellow pupils to spy upon them. Puffing after their exertions, Sam and John beached the boat and stretched out lazily on the sandy soil.

"We forgot the fishing poles." Sam sighed. "Oh well, there'll be turtle eggs."

A few minutes later they were thrusting their fingers into the sand, which was warm at the top, less warm and somewhat moist below. "Look at this big one!" cried John, and Sam soon brought up five smaller eggs that a mother turtle had covered over.

Carefully they gathered bits of twigs and paper. They had brought along two of the newfangled "lucifer matches." Most people still used flint to draw a spark, but with matches a fire could be started much more easily, almost magically. The boys blew and blew and nursed the tiny flame. Only when it was burning well could they relax again.

Putting their eggs to bake in the ashes, they went off to explore the island. They ran after screaming water birds, dug deep pits in the sand, and tried to track down shadowy animals in the grass. "It's almost like being Robinson Crusoe," Sam told John.

Here was a world in itself, complete and exciting. Downriver, around New Orleans and the Gulf of Mexico, Sam had heard that magnificent alligators crawled along the Mississippi. They were the only things that Glasscock's Island lacked. When he got bigger, Sam assured himself, he would see those alligators.

Much later the boys discovered that dusk was approaching; they had been exploring longer than they planned. Taking up their eggs, they tossed them from hand to hand until they cooled a trifle, and swallowed them hurriedly. A few minutes later they started their long row across the river.

Toward midstream Sam and John made out a pale shape rolling steadily and rapidly toward them. It was one of the biggest of the steamboats. For a moment they peered up in admiration. "What a boat that is," Sam whispered.

But both of them knew what massive waves a steam vessel made, and hastily they rowed on toward shore to get out of its path. Even after they reached a place of safety, they felt the great lift and fall of the water.

Now the blue-gray shadows were everywhere, and as they beached the boat and started home Sam told himself that his family must have missed him long ago. He felt reluctant to face the thrashing he was sure to get for being late. Suppose he went instead to the little office in which his father carried on his duties? At least he would put off punishment. In the case of punishment, Sam always liked to postpone matters as long as possible.

In the early dusk Sam lifted the office window and lowered himself inside. After a few minutes, his eyes became accustomed to the dimness and he recognized vague, familiar shapes: the outline of a boxlike desk, a picture on the wall. Then his gaze went to the floor, and his frame stiffened. Was he imagining it or did he see a new object, without a clear shape but long and stretched out? Could it be a body?

Sam felt goose bumps rise at the back of his neck and move down his spine. Shivering, he turned to the wall. Immediately he realized that if the thing on the floor reached over, it could seize him when his back was turned.

Swinging around, Sam faced the shape below him. The more he looked, the more it appeared to be a human figure. Minutes passed, seeming like hours. Soon the moonlight would be coming through the window to illuminate the scene, but could he manage to wait?

In despair Sam decided that the moon would never show itself that evening. Turning around again, he blinked at the wall and started counting. But before he reached twenty, his anxiety about the dark object returned. He shifted his position so that he could look toward it. A pale square of moonlight showed on the carpet. Now it almost touched the thing.

Desperately Sam made himself stare at the wall and count again: "One, two, three . . ." This time he managed to reach one hundred. Then, swinging around once more, he saw—a white hand. He felt as if he were nailed to the sofa. Who was it—a stranger or someone Sam knew—and what was he doing there?

With a hard, new effort Sam gathered strength to turn to the wall again. "One, two . . ." Trembling more than ever, he managed to reach one hundred twenty-five.

Then he opened his eyes and looked down upon a cold gray face, the corners of the mouth pulled down, the eyes open and gleaming like a pair of hard marbles. He gaped at the corpse as the light continued to advance across its bare chest, a little at a time. Sam almost cried out as he saw a deep gash made by some murderer.

That was enough for him. "I went away from there," he wrote later. "I do not say that I went away in any sort of a hurry. . . . I went out at the window, and I carried the sash along with me; I did not need the sash, but it was handier to take it than it was to leave it. . . ." He added, "I was not scared, but I was considerably agitated."

Although his father whipped him when he reached home, Sam remembered that he "enjoyed it." Anything, anything at all was better than remaining in the room with that figure stretched upon the floor.

Later he discovered what had happened. While he had been gallivanting about on the river, there had been a public murder, which some of his friends had seen. Had he stayed in town, he might have witnessed all the excitement. Two farmers had come to Hannibal and begun to argue over a new plow in a store. One pulled out a knife and thrust it into his friend. Within a few minutes the victim gasped his final breath. As justice of the peace, Judge Clemens would have to hold a hearing with the corpse on view, and there was nowhere else to place it until the next day except his office.

When bedtime arrived, Sam took two of his cats with him for company. But he could not put away his recollection of that grim moonlit scene at his father's office, and he slept very little that night.

6

Epidemic

In the spring of 1844 an epidemic of measles swept through Hannibal and several children died. Fathers and mothers became frantic and gave strict orders to their children to stay indoors. For the lively Sam, this was especially difficult. Day after day he fidgeted in the narrow hallway, the kitchen, and the room he shared with Henry.

Every now and then he felt a chill and told himself happily: "There, I have it, and I'll die and not have to worry about things like epidemics." But he caught nothing. Sam thought that this kind of uncertain life was not worth living, and finally he decided to try to get the disease and have it over with, one way or the other.

When word arrived a day or two later that his

good friend Will Bowen lay ill, Sam told himself he would pay the sick boy a call. Creeping away from the house, he went to Will's, tiptoing upstairs so that no one would see him. But just as he entered his friend's room, Will's mother walked in. Shaking her finger in his face, she gave him a stiff scolding. Although Sam had to leave, he had not been defeated. He would simply be more careful the next time.

He stood for nearly an hour behind the Bowen house, peeping through a crack in the fence. At last the coast was clear. He sped up the back stairway and joined Will in bed. As a conversationalist, however, Will proved a sad disappointment. He was so sick that he did not even know Sam was there.

Sam jumped in alarm when footsteps sounded outside the door. It was Mrs. Bowen again. His heart pounding, he drew the sheet over his head. But it was no use. "Sammy, get up this minute!" she ordered. With a firm hand on his collar she pulled him out, and never let go until she had taken him downstairs, led him through the streets, and turned him over to Mrs. Clemens herself.

Sam's second stay with Will had done the trick, however. Soon afterward he went to his own bed with a severe case of measles. Lying there peacefully, Sam had no interest in anything. "I have never enjoyed anything in my life any more than I enjoyed dying that time," he later wrote. Word went out to the Quarles farm and to other family connections and they assembled, he said, to "see me off." While his relatives cried and shook their heads, Sam felt rather pleased. After all, he was the center of their excitement.

Toward the end, the doctor put bags of hot ashes over his chilled body, on his chest, wrists, and ankles. To his own astonishment, Sam said, the medical man dragged him back into the world.

Soon Sam was back at the river landing with his friends. One boy, Jack, was missing. He had left Hannibal and for months his friends heard nothing of him. Occasionally they wondered what he was doing. Sam was sitting one afternoon at the landing, watching the approaching steamboat. He was struck speechless when he saw Jack himself, leaning over the railing of the deck.

Sam called to him, and proudly Jack explained that he had a job as a "striker," an apprentice engineer. "Oh, it's grand work—fine people in the crew, and all the passengers. And you're in a new place every few hours, you know."

With every word Jack rubbed fresh salt into Sam's wounds. It wasn't right, Sam told himself. The fellow was part of that exalted world of the river, and here *he* was, miserable and unnoticed. From then on, every time the steamboat arrived, Jack was cleaning

49

a rusty bolt or doing some other chore in a spot where no one could miss him. Sometimes the boat was laid up for a few hours at Hannibal. Then Jack would take still more of the spotlight by strutting through the streets in his greasiest clothes, so that everybody would know of his connection with a steamboat.

When he spoke he threw in every steamboat term he knew—referring to the "labboard side" of a horse, or a building that stood "upriver." He appeared to have forgotten everyday talk, and he did it all in so easy and natural a way, Sam said, that the rest of them almost hoped he would die.

Then, one day startling news sped through Hannibal. Jack's steamboat had blown up in the river, and reports said that he had been lost in the wreckage. Sam and his friends declared solemnly that they were sorry, very sorry.

But the fellow would *not* be killed, even by a steam disaster. Jack showed up very much alive the next week, and on Sunday went to church covered with bruises, red marks, and bandages. Everybody stared, everybody asked questions, everybody congratulated Jack. Sam gritted his teeth. Why should heaven let such good things happen to so unworthy a reptile as Jack?

More than ever, every boy in Hannibal set his eyes on the river. Sam watched sadly as one after another, the older youths left to work on the steamboats. One month the minister's son appeared as a full-fledged engineer. The postmaster's boy and the doctor's emerged as "mud clerks," assistants without any pay except for room and board on the boat, and the chance to become a full-fledged clerk. Two sons of the county judge even rose to the exalted position of pilot. Sam fretted; would there be any place left for him?

Asking questions at the Mississippi landing, he learned more about piloting. A pilot earned $150 to $250 a month, with free bed and board—a magnificent wage for the times. "Why," Sam informed Henry, "two months' pay on the river gives a man more than a minister gets in a year." More than ever, he wanted to be a part of the riverboat life.

One day a steamboat was delayed for two hours at Hannibal. Here was Sam's chance to ask for a job. His heart thumping in his chest, the boy walked boldly up the gangplank.

"I'd like to see the pilot," he informed the first official-looking person he encountered.

"You would, would you? See him about what?" The man frowned down at Sam.

"The thing is," the boy confided, "I want to be a pilot myself."

That sounded businesslike and important to Sam, but the listener did not seem to agree. He slapped his

51

knee and chuckled hard. "Come back in fifteen years, sonny. When you get grown up." The man pointed to the gangplank and, his face burning red, Sam marched down it.

But his determination did not leave him. More than ever, he yearned to ride a steamboat and see the world along the Mississippi. He just couldn't stay cooped up on the riverbank like this. If he could not be a pilot, he would take a place as a water carrier, a boy member of the crew. A bit later he spied several youths on the deck of one of the vessels and tried to talk with them.

"Any chance of getting a job like yours?" he asked the boy nearest him.

"A job for who?"

"For me."

"A runt like *you*?" The youth turned away coldly.

Sam gave up the thought for several days. Then he remembered something: the excitement that occurred when one of the big boats reached the landing. That would be the right moment to slip on, hide in a good spot, and watch what happened. Since he would not have any fare, they would have to give him work so he could earn his way.

Why hadn't he thought of it before? Already he had lost years that he might have been enjoying on a steamboat. That same afternoon, saying not a word to any of the family, Sam took a place just behind two big men and stepped aboard. No one noticed him as he followed the pair to the upper deck.

Now he must find a place to hide. He spotted a lifeboat along the railing, jumped under it, and sat down out of sight, barely breathing. Soon the signal bell sounded, and he felt the engines rolling under him. He had watched the scene so often from shore, and now at last he was part of it.

Out there lay Hannibal, his home, disappearing into the distance. For a moment Sam suffered a pang of regret. Should he have left a note at the house? Well, he would write a message somewhere on the way and have it sent back to the family.

For a few moments everything went as he had planned. Then Sam jumped as he felt water beating on him from one side. A heavy shower had started. He drew back, huddling beneath the boat, but he could not get away from the water. Some of the glamour of the adventure began to trickle away with the drops. Then all at once Sam realized that two men were standing a few inches away from him.

"Right here."

"Must be a boy."

Too late Sam realized that his feet had been showing. Before he could pull them in, two pairs of strong arms pulled him out. Angry eyes focused on him, and their owners asked him a lot of questions.

"I—I just got on in Hannibal," Sam stammered. "I want a job on the boat, any job you have."

The men scowled. One of them shook his head. "You're getting right off at the next landing."

The other man rubbed his mustache. "Aren't you Judge Clemens's son?"

There was no use in denying the truth.

"Yes, sir."

"Well," the man smiled a little, "the next stop happens to be the town of Louisiana, and the judge once told me he has a relative there. I'll see that he hears you've arrived."

Sam's heart sank. Dolefully he sat on the deck, watching the riverbank slide by in the rain. He had scarcely expected so disheartening and quick an ending to his voyage. The settlement came into view; the mate clamped his fingers on the boy's arm and led him down the gangplank as several people snickered.

At the landing the mate talked seriously to one of the townspeople and gave the boy into his protection. "Your cousin will take you back on the next boat," the stranger said. "Don't worry about anything." Unable to speak, Sam wondered how his father and mother would feel about this, and what the people of Hannibal would say.

When he reached home the following day, Mrs. Clemens ran out, arms extended, eyes full of tears.

"Sammy, you're alive! We didn't know what to think, or where to turn."

His father waited at the window, arms folded and vigorous disapproval on his lean face. It would be weeks before Sam heard the end of this. Nevertheless, he said to himself, he would be riding along the river someday, and the next time he would not have to sneak aboard.

To his surprise, he discovered himself a hero among the boys of the village. They had all talked at one time or another of a feat such as his, but it had taken Sam Clemens to achieve it. "It wasn't your fault they caught you," said Tom Blankenship. Sam glowed inside. Praise from Tom was high praise indeed.

Tom Blankenship and Will Bowen and several others were with Sam in an adventure of another sort. It was a murder—the first Sam had ever seen. Violence of this kind was not uncommon as the river traffic made Hannibal more and more a bustling town.

For years Sam had known Mr. Sam Smarr, an elderly, good-natured farmer who had one failing. Occasionally Mr. Smarr went to one of the barrooms near the river and came out staggering. In that condition Mr. Smarr would go around town, shouting and threatening to "fix" this or that individual. Sam had watched while the bigger boys jeered at him. He had heard several people remark: "Poor Mr. Smarr, he's not really dangerous. With all his threats, he'd never hurt anybody in the least."

The boy was also acquainted with Mr. William Owsley, a well-to-do businessman who was always handsomely dressed. The people in Hannibal thought him a bit proud. One day Mr. Smarr arrived in town and Sam noticed him walk unsteadily past Mr. Owsley's store. "Bill Owsley's a thief," Smarr yelled, "a man that's stolen things from a lot of folks, and I'm going to get him yet."

Presently old Mr. Smarr went away, but Sam heard others whisper that Mr. Owsley was "real mad, and silentlike—the worst kind of a way to be mad." Several days later, Sam was leaning against a post near his house when he noticed Mr. Smarr and another farmer talking together. Then suddenly the boy saw Mr. Owsley come up behind them, a strange look on his whitened face.

Something told Sam that real trouble was about to happen. Mr. Owsley pulled out a pistol, and Mr. Smarr turned around.

"Don't shoot me!" he cried. As Sam and several companions watched, Mr. Owsley fired twice and Mr. Smarr dropped to the street.

Mr. Owsley strode off, and someone ran for a doctor. While a crowd gathered, the friend carried the injured farmer into a store next door. Biting his lips, Sam asked himself: Was Mr. Smarr really going to die? A half-hour passed, and then Mr. Smarr's head dropped back in death.

Sam was frightened. The men in the crowd had all liked Mr. Smarr, and all at once they were mumbling to one another, "We ought to hang that stuck-up fellow." "Get a rope!" "Let's do it right now!"

Before Sam Clemens's eyes, a raging mob formed and pushed on toward Mr. Owsley's house. The boy did not want to watch what followed but he was caught by the horror of it, and he let the crowd thrust him forward. A short time afterward he stared nervously as the mob clustered before the Owsley home, one member waving a heavy rope.

Then Mr. Owsley stepped forth from his second-floor window to the roof of the porch and stared down at them.

"You're a bunch of cowards," Mr. Owsley shouted. "All of you against one man." He had a double-barreled gun in his hand and he pointed it toward one member of the mob and then another. As he did, each man trembled and jumped away. Mr. Owsley faced them down, one by one. Finally he raised his voice again: "Get out! Get off my property."

The mob fell back and began to disappear down the street. The danger to Mr. Owsley had ended.

Months later the case went to trial and Mr. Owsley

was declared not guilty. To the townspeople, however, his action was unforgivable, and they did not hesitate to let him know how they felt. The merchant was eventually forced to move away.

As for young Sam Clemens, he never forgot the tense scene when Owsley faced the irate crowd, and he later described it in *The Adventures of Huckleberry Finn*.

A Real
Steamboat Ride

One morning Judge Clemens glanced up from his breakfast and asked, "Sam, would you like to take a trip with me?"

Nine-year-old Sam loved travel anywhere at any time, and he said yes without even asking any questions. Judge Clemens went on: "We'll go by steamboat down to St. Louis on business. I have to see some supply people and—"

Sam missed the rest of his father's words. Mrs. Clemens almost dropped a plate of corn cakes as Sam shouted and did a dance around the table. She sighed. "Sammy, it's nice that your father can take you, but does it mean all *that* much?"

It did. For the next five nights he slept irregularly and in the daytime did little except tell his friends about "the trip I'll be taking down to St. Louis." Some of them were envious, as envious as Sam himself had been of the Hannibal boys who joined the steamboat ranks.

"The trip's an overnight one, you understand," Sam said again and again, although every youth in town knew that. "But before I go to sleep that night, I'm going to look over every part of the boat. Anything you'd like me to find out for you?" He did not mind rubbing his friends' noses in his glory.

On the afternoon of the trip, Sam jumped on the stage plank as soon as it connected with the landing, and raced aboard before anyone else. After a time, with Judge Clemens at his side he inspected the lower deck, staring at the dozens of perspiring laborers and poorly dressed passengers—most of them emigrants from Europe or from older American states.

Later Sam went upstairs where the more elite passengers sat about playing cards and listening to music—the women in one parlor, the men in another. For the boy it was a dazzling place, strange and elegant and beautiful like nothing else in the world.

Briefly Sam's father took him to the well-scrubbed, well-polished pilothouse, where they shook hands with a man who was very busy at the wheel, and his assistant. Sam wanted to stay up there a long time. "But they're mighty occupied, son," Judge Clemens explained, "and we'd only be in the way." Regretfully Sam followed his father from the pilothouse.

For the boy it was an evening of glory. When supper time arrived he found that everything tasted better than it did on land. The attendants, amused at his intense interest, served him a large bowl of thick soup and then another one, part of a great stuffed fish, sizzling pieces of meat—and two desserts. He could have had six desserts if he wished, for the steamboat had long lines of them. But Judge Clemens said that two were enough. "One too many, in fact."

Sam stayed up far later than usual, and his father had difficulty in getting him to his cabin. At one point in the evening, several people mentioned a terrible steamboat explosion that had just occurred near New Orleans. Men had been thrown into the air, others trapped in the burning half of the vessel. "The worst in years . . . Women jumped into the water and were drowned with babies in their arms." Such words were the last the boy heard as he retired.

It had been an exciting day and Sam could hardly sleep. After a great deal of effort, however, he managed to doze. All at once he sat up in his berth. He was never certain what happened, but he thought he saw a flame through his window and heard someone shout: "Boilers exploding!"

Sam leaped from his berth. He had to warn the

passengers of their danger. His nightshirt swinging around his thin legs, he dashed out of the cabin. In the parlor near his door were about twenty-five women, reading and sewing. Eyes wide, his hair standing on end, Sam cried: "Fire, fire! Jump and run; you don't have a minute to lose!"

To his astonishment all of them looked up calmly, revealing no sign of disturbance. Several gave gentle smiles, and the most elderly of all drew her spectacles down on her nose and murmured sweetly: "You mustn't catch cold, child. Run and put something on, and then tell us about it."

Sam collapsed in shame. He had been certain that the passengers would hail him as their savior from a horrible death. Instead they were making fun of him. Humbly he crept back to his cabin. In the morning he hurried off the vessel with his father, taking care to avoid the glances of the women.

Sam's eyes had been turning more and more often of late toward a certain pretty girl who sat near him in school. When his brother Henry teased him about it, Mrs. Clemens told him to "let Sammy alone."

"Before long you'll be paying heed to them yourself," she said. Snorting at that foolish remark, Henry sped off to more important concerns, like marble-shooting and kite-flying.

The girl's name was Laura Hawkins, and she was

two years younger than Sam. A soft-faced blonde with light blue eyes, Laura wore calico and had her hair plaited into a pair of long pigtails that hung beneath her sunbonnet. Many years later, when he wrote *Tom Sawyer,* Sam used her as a model for Becky Thatcher. Laura's uncle operated the new ferry that ran between Hannibal and the Illinois side of the river. The Hawkins family had moved into a house at Hill and Main streets, close to the Clemenses, and the two families were good neighbors.

By this time, boys and girls of Sam's age were going on picnics along the Mississippi or up Holliday's Hill. And now and then they took the Hawkins's ferryboat downriver to favorite picnicking spots under the oaks. At times, too, there were candy pulls and apple-bobbing parties.

Meeting Laura on the way to school, Sam would carry her books and her lunch basket. She frequently gave him an apple or a piece of cake, and he repaid her with a handful of berries from the woods. During his summers at the Quarles farm, he had learned to locate them in places that few people knew about.

"Why, Sam, I didn't realize these berries were out yet," Laura would tell him, and he would flush with pride.

One day Laura came along when he was building a small house of bricks. "Help me finish it," Sam invited and the girl went to work, lifting and piling the bricks in even lines until one fell on her hand. He caught her fingers to soothe the pain, and Laura began to cry. To her surprise, the sympathetic Sam wept with her.

After a time he provided a stronger demonstration of his feelings for Laura. Although never a good student, he had developed an interest in spelling. Every Friday afternoon at school Mr. Cross held a spelling bee. Sam liked to be in the spotlight and he enjoyed the congratulations that showered upon him when he spelled down another student. Friday was one day when he never played hooky.

Once, however, he faced Laura in a match. She and Sam were deadlocked as the contest approached its end. No matter how much Sam yearned to shine, he didn't welcome the prospect of defeating the girl. Mr. Cross called out: "Spell the second month of the year."

Swiftly Sam started: "F–E–B . . ." He hesitated, then completed the word: "U–A–R–Y."

"That's wrong. Laura, will you try?"

With a look of pride Laura sang out, "F–E–B–*R*–U–A–R–Y."

"Correct, absolutely correct!" Mr. Cross was pleased, and Sam himself beamed as Laura took the spelling medal. He had known there were two *R*'s in the word and had made the mistake on purpose—all for Laura Hawkins.

Mr. Cross bestowed another medal on Fridays, but Sam Clemens never received it. It was the award for good behavior. A week after Sam lost to Laura, however, he managed to earn the spelling medal for himself. When his friend John Robards won the one for behavior, Sam had a bright thought. "Why don't we swap them for a while?" he asked, and John agreed. As Sam paraded around with the medal for fine behavior, many who knew him marveled. What miracle was going to happen next?

One of those who looked at him in surprise was Mr. Cross himself. The teacher soon did more than look. He took the medals away from both boys.

Although Sam's closest friends were Will Bowen and John Briggs, other boys earned his admiration for one reason or another. One was Jimmy McDaniel. Jimmy was popular in Hannibal because his family owned a candy store. All the other boys wished they had been born in his place. "You know," Sam told John Briggs, "I'll bet he eats candy all the time, breakfast, dinner, and supper."

Jimmy insisted that he seldom tasted the stuff. "I don't bother about it because it's there all the time," he announced grandly.

The observant Sam thought he had evidence that Jimmy was lying. "Look." Sam nudged John. "He's got the very worst teeth in town." Still, there wasn't one boy in Hannibal who would not have changed places with Jimmy, bad teeth and all.

Second in general admiration, and for a special reason, was John Robards, the same youth who had won the good behavior medal. He was a slender boy with very long, very straight, very light hair, which hung like a curtain at each side of his face. This hair was an object of envy to Sam, whose short reddish curls would never lie down on his head. As John worked over his slate, one section of his hair would slip down into his eyes. With that he would toss his head, the way a pony does, and throw it back.

A few minutes later John would toss his head the opposite way. And each time nearly everybody would glance up. Sam suspected that the boy did this mainly to show off. But he knew that if he could have managed such a feat, he would have done it in exactly the same fashion.

A third boy possessed another distinction: he could make his ears go back and forth like a horse's. One other member of the class, however, had a particularly magnificent gift. He could make his big toe double back and crack so hard that people heard it twenty yards away. In the winter, this richly talented fellow had to wear shoes like most of the others, and his great talent was concealed. But every summer the cracking of the boy's toe was heard far and wide and, said the jealous Sam, he was "a bitterness to us."

On Sundays, Mrs. Clemens sent Sam to evening church services. Knowing her older son, she often tested him to find out if he had really attended. When he returned she would ask: "What was the text?" For several months she nodded with pleasure as Sam told her—each time a fine, different text. This arrangement worked well until a neighbor dropped in and happened to mention the subject the minister had used that evening. "Why, Sammy, that's not the one you told me about!" his mother cried. Even Sam had no explanation this time.

One icy night Sam set out for church wearing his long black cloak. Leaving the house, he tossed it aside and joined the other boys in a game for an hour or so, then started back home. He did not notice, alas, that he had put the cloak on inside out, its bright plaid lining showing.

"How was the service, Sammy?" his mother inquired. "Who was there?" As he answered her questions, he did not notice the trap Mrs. Clemens was setting for him. She continued: "It must have been hard to keep warm there on such a cold night."

Sam gave an airy wave of his hand. "Oh, I kept my cloak on all the time."

"And on the way back, too?"

That was an easy one, Sam thought. "Oh, yes."

Jane Clemens gave her son a piercing look. "Then you must have made a real show, with all those colors flashing in people's faces." Caught, Sam gulped and sat silent. The next Sunday he made certain that he attended.

8

Boys on the Prowl

As the New Year approached, friends advised Sam to make a resolution to "turn over a new leaf" by starting a diary and writing in it every night. In that way, they assured him, he would become a new boy, and a better one. Not very enthusiastically, Sam agreed to try and began bravely on the first evening.

"Monday: Got up, washed, went to bed."

That was all he could think of. Well, the next night might be better, Sam told himself. This time he pondered over the diary for many minutes and put down: "Tuesday: Got up, washed, went to bed." So it went for Wednesday, Thursday, and Friday. Two Fridays later he was still writing: "Got up, washed, went to bed."

Sighing, Sam gave up the whole project. The trouble, he decided, was that so few exciting events happened to him. But looking over the pages, he remarked that he was proud to find himself so well washed.

Despite what Sam claimed, lively events were going on around him, and he had a full part in them. Nearly every day the river and its banks called the boys of the town to activities in which not even Laura Hawkins was welcome. They ranged farther and farther from Hannibal, engaging in ever more adventurous deeds. And more frequently than before, Sam's companion was the carefree Tom Blankenship.

Mrs. Clemens worried about their friendship. She would ask: "Who's going along today?" Sam would shrug. "Oh, just Will Bowen and John Briggs and maybe one or two others." "One or two others" generally meant Tom. The older youth, who knew the river and the woods better than anyone in town, understood Jane Clemens's feelings. So he arranged a secret system of communication with Sam.

From some nearby point Tom would make a sound like a bird or an animal, perhaps the meow of a cat. Hearing it, Sam would excuse himself from his unsuspecting family and leave the house. Tom Blankenship occasionally gave his call after Sam had gone upstairs for the night. In such cases he left the house by a secret route. From the window of his room he dropped noiselessly to a one-story back roof; from there he dropped again to an arbor with many vines, and finally to the ground. An hour or two later he climbed up the same way, and no one was the wiser.

During these excursions the boys wandered in the woods or climbed to the top of Holliday's Hill, from which they could look over the town and the Mississippi as if they owned them. Most days they ended up on the river itself. Sometimes they used sails for their borrowed boats, but more often they rowed. Their years on the Mississippi had given them real skill, and they could cover the water in a boat almost as fast as they could run on land.

On their way down to the river, the gang learned where the finest orchards waited and where the best melons nestled in the fields. Invariably they gathered a few pieces of fruit to be enjoyed while they lolled at the river edge or on Glasscock's Island. From home one of them brought bacon for frying over their fire, and they fished for bass and perch and river catfish. The fishing became a contest, in which the boy who drew the biggest catch won the honors—until someone took them from him on the next outing.

From their favorite Glasscock's Island, the distance back to the Missouri side was only a half-mile. They took delight in swimming it, testing their muscles against the currents of Old Man Mississippi and watching out for paddle-wheelers and big flatboats.

Although he was not the oldest, eleven-year-old Sam was taking more and more leadership in their play. More energetic than most, he also had more imagination. He was continually thinking of new paths to explore and new ways to amuse the gang. He liked bright costumes—bandit hats, eye patches, colorful sashes.

Playing Robin Hood was a favorite sport. The boys would dart about the woods in their shirttails, hiding from one another. At a signal, a scattered band would swoop noisily into action, thrusting and parrying with their wooden swords, and going through the motions of "robbing the rich to help the poor."

As they lolled contentedly on the riverbank, the boys argued about their ambitions. "The best thing in the world," one of them would say, "is to be a river bandit, holding up the boats that pass and taking all their gold, and then hiding in the woods."

Another youth disagreed. "It would be a lot better to work like old man Murrell and organize secret followers everywhere. Brotherhoods of crime—that's it! And we'd lurk along the Natchez Trace, behind a bush, with guns to halt anybody that went by."

A third boy nodded his head. "Oh, we'd give 'em a fair chance—their money or their lives. We wouldn't shoot unless we had to," he added generously.

A few of the band wanted to become trappers.

"We'd be away from people for weeks at a time, maybe dealing with just a few Indians. And we'd get to know bears and wolves the way we know the people next door." It sounded very exciting.

But most of the boys finally agreed—and Sam most of all—that the best occupation was piloting on the Mississippi. To take one's place behind the wheel of a steamboat—nothing, nothing on earth could match it.

Sam had become one of the best swimmers in the area. Even now, however, he frequently missed disaster by narrow margins.

One windy day when he was riding on a ferry, a storm threatened the area. Just as they reached the center of the river, his hat blew off. Perhaps because there were girls in the crowd looking on, Sam decided he had to get it back. He stepped to the top of the rail and jumped into the water.

The current was very strong, and he had to swim hard toward the hat, which bobbed up and down on the surface. The ferry stopped, and promptly a crowd gathered on the shore. People called to the boy, although he could barely hear even those closest to him. "Come back, come back!" "Forget that hat, do you hear?"

Sam had no intention of doing either; his honor demanded that he carry through. Foamy whitecaps lifted and fell as the wind whined over the gray Mississippi. For a time people could not make out the boy's head in the water, and some of them gave him up for lost. "That's where he went down. . . ." "Poor Sam's gone," they began to whisper.

But Sam fought the powerful Mississippi. Gradually, swimming with every ounce of his power, he forced his way back to safety. The hat was clutched in his hand. The crowd cheered, and then bustled him into dry clothes, telling him he had been a "young fool." Still, Sam found himself a hero, and the new sensation delighted him through and through.

Inevitably there was tragedy on the Mississippi, and it touched Sam's life. A boy named Clint, who had been skylarking on an old flatboat, jumped too high and fell in. "Being loaded with sin," Sam later wrote, "he went to the bottom like an anvil," and could not be brought up in time.

That night Sam was sure that the dead young man was "the only boy in the village who slept." Sam and the others lay awake hour after hour, thinking of what had happened, and repenting of their own sins. A violent thunderstorm struck after dark and roared on until dawn, the wind whining, windows shaking, and streams of rain raging against the Clemens house.

Repeatedly Sam shuddered as bolts of lightning cut through the night, turning everything into glaring whiteness. He sat up in bed, trembling, "waiting for the destruction of the world, and expecting it." This was a special judgment on him, he felt certain.

He was going to be "in the fire" with his friend Clint. Desperately trying to draw attention from himself, Sam began to pray. In his prayers he mentioned other boys who, he claimed, had behaved even worse than he had. One had broken a window and fibbed about it. Another fished on Sunday, claimed he had caught only a tiny mudcat, then said he threw it back—but hadn't!

Suddenly Sam realized that in his fright he had left the candle lighted, making it easier for the angry spirits to discover him. Hastily he jumped from under the covers and blew out the flame. With his head covered again, he made a long and strong resolution: If lightning did not hit him tonight, he would become a new boy.

He would go regularly to church, he said. He would call on the sick, give stern lectures to his friends, and suffer quietly when they thrashed him for doing so. He would bring baskets to the poor, though he suspected that even the poorest people in Hannibal would be furious if he tried that and would break the baskets over his head.

Eventually sleep overcame Sam. The next day, when he found that nobody had been struck by lightning, his alarm faded away, and he went back to his usual pursuits.

A little later there came another tragedy for Sam and his friends. Among their group was a German boy, nicknamed Dutchy. Dutchy was so well-behaved at all times that he made Sam furious. One Sunday morning this model boy amazed everybody by reciting dozens of verses of scripture perfectly. But the very next day he was drowned.

That night another bad storm hit Hannibal. Alone in his room, Sam felt more doomed than before. If a boy like Dutchy, who knew all those Bible verses, became a victim, what hope was there for someone like *him*? Once again he promised that he would be a new Sam, an upright one. But just as before, the sun finally came out, breakfast time arrived, and he and his companions slid back into their old ways.

For a long time the greatest adventure for Sam and the rest of the gang was a visit to McDowell's Cave, a wonderful cavity in the earth along the river, about three miles below Hannibal. Here was a place about which Missourians told a hundred tales—about its mysteries, its natural marvels, the dangerous secrets it held.

The cave had miles of passages, wide and narrow, connecting and interconnecting. Many of them ended in great echoing chambers. People gossiped about this or that person who had experienced the slimmest of escapes, getting out only after being lost for days.

Certain hapless individuals, it was said, never came out at all. They became hopelessly lost and collapsed from fatigue, hunger, and terror, dying by slow degrees.

Everywhere inside hung stalactites, icicle-shaped formations extending down from the roof. They reminded Sam of the hands of ghosts. To members of the band, McDowell's Cave had obviously been the scene of villainous deeds performed in ancient times.

"I'll bet a lot of river pirates used to hide here," Sam speculated.

"They concealed their gold inside," Will Bowen agreed, "and dragged their victims here to torture them."

To the gang, old "Injun Joe" served as a kind of patron saint of McDowell's Cave. An elderly man, he lazed around Hannibal, sometimes drunken and rowdy, but causing no harm to anybody. The boys believed there was a certain mystery about Joe and whenever they saw him they felt a vague fear.

Townspeople told of the time Injun Joe had been lost in the cave for days. He had managed to survive only by killing bats and eating them. At last he staggered out, hollow-chested, with a mark of horror on him. The story haunted Sam Clemens and many years later he used it in *Tom Sawyer*.

Often Sam and his friends broke into small groups to explore McDowell's Cave. Taking candles, they crept along the winding tomblike passages. The candles threw flickering shadows on the walls, making a hand appear like a claw that reached out to snatch them and carry them off.

When they called to one another, their voices echoed and re-echoed down the vast rocky corridors. At times a slight wind stirred inside the earth, as if from some newly opened grave, and suddenly a candle would go out. Then the boys would yell to other members of their party who were following different routes. Sometimes they received only silence for a reply.

"Do you think they've forgotten us?" Will Bowen would ask. And Sam would wonder if they were doomed to stay there for the rest of their lives.

On one occasion when they were lost in this way, they had only a single candle, which was melting fast. They shouted for what seemed hours until finally they heard Tom Blankenship's reply: "Hey, Sam, and the rest of you!" Tom's voice had never sounded more welcome.

At times like this, Sam would vow never again to enter the dark cavern. A few days later, however, Tom would ask, "Who wants to go to McDowell's Cave?" and Sam would jump up before anyone else.

9

Turning Point

For months eleven-year-old Sam, Tom Blankenship, and their friends had been enjoying a lively new sport. They would climb to the top of Holliday's Hill, hunt for large rocks, pry them loose, and roll them down the slope. The boys usually picked a Sunday, when dozens of carriages and wagons passed. Hidden among trees and bushes, they would watch eagerly as the boulders rolled on their way.

"It's going to hit the wheel of that red one!" Tom would yell.

"Missed it!" Will Bowen would cry. "But I'll bet it gets the little wagon right behind it."

The rocks seldom struck anything or, if they did, caused little damage. Nevertheless, the boys watched gleefully as vehicles halted and men jumped out in a rage to shake their fists at the unseen youths. Eventually this happened too often, and word leaked out that the town officials were going to try to catch them.

"We'd better lie low for a while," Sam cautioned, and for weeks the boys stayed away from the hilltop. After the alarm died down, he had a new thought. "Why don't we give them a real show—a last big thrill?" he asked.

"How?" two of the boys asked at the same time.

"Look." Sam pointed to an enormous boulder, almost the size of a wagon, rising above their heads.

"Wonderful," said Tom Blankenship. "But we'd never be able to pry it loose."

"We could if we worked hard enough," Sam replied. "But I suppose you fellows don't really have your hearts in it."

His challenging words had their effect. Each member of the band was ready to do the deed, no matter how long it took. They now labored steadily through each weekend. Luckily bushes shielded the rock, and nobody noticed them.

A short distance below, laborers had been working for weeks to cut rock from the hill, and every Sunday the boys borrowed their picks and shovels. The boulder lay deep in the earth, and as they struggled they developed dozens of blisters on their hands. Would they ever get it done?

They did, unexpectedly. Early one Sunday the rock began to move, almost falling on two of the boys. "It's coming," Sam called out, and they jumped to one side. Fascinated, the gang gaped as the missile rolled down the slope. Like all falling objects, it gathered momentum on the way.

Halfway down the hill, the boulder hit a tree and wrecked it completely. Sam whistled. Who would have thought it could do a thing like that? The crash sent the boulder in a slightly different direction. A short distance below, a man driving a cart was directly in its path. Glancing up, he shouted, whipped his horse, and tried to get out of the way.

"It's going to smash the cart!" Sam cried.

Then, a few feet from the vehicle, the rock hit a small obstruction and went sailing through the air. It missed the cart—but now it was moving swiftly upon a cooper's shop. As the boys watched, the boulder crashed into the side of the wooden building.

"Say, we'd better get out of here!" Tom Blankenship whispered.

Sam was already on his way. The band scattered in several directions. Nobody was going to catch any of them near the scene. They were not seen together again until two or three days later, when they agreed unanimously that they had pushed their last boulder down the hill.

*   *   *

81

The Clemens family's fortunes grew worse in 1846. Sam's father had endorsed a loan made to a man who owned many properties in town. Judge Clemens did not realize that the man almost never paid his debts. For months the subject was disputed. Then one day the Clemens family found they had lost everything they possessed.

They were forced to move in with the Grant family who lived above a drugstore. In exchange for their rooms, Mrs. Clemens would provide board for the Grants. Never had things appeared so bad. Sam had little to say about the matter, but he brooded over it. At night he had dreams of vague, disturbing forces that hovered above the house. What was going to happen to them?

Then matters brightened, at least a little. Several friends paid a call on Judge Clemens, urging him to run for clerk of court, in an election to be held in August 1847. The general respect with which the town regarded the judge began to show itself. Members of both political parties supported him, and everybody agreed that Sam's father would win.

The boy saw Mrs. Clemens's spirits improve. "All we have to do is hold out until summer's over," she told Sam. "After that everything will be better."

March started, a cold, windy month. Judge Clemens left Hannibal on legal business, and on the way home he was caught in sleet and rain. When Sam opened the door that night, his father stood drenched, his face almost blue with cold. Mrs. Clemens sent him right to bed, and prepared several of her many medicines.

In the morning Judge Clemens had a drawn look and coughed a great deal. He had always been thin, but recently he had lost weight. A few days later the doctor drew Mrs. Clemens aside and talked very seriously with her. He was afraid the judge had pneumonia, and a serious case of it. By steamboat a message was sent to Sam's older brother, Orion, in St. Louis, and Orion soon returned to Hannibal.

Sam went around the house on tiptoe. "We have to do everything we can for Pa," Orion said, and Sam nodded. Although his condition did not improve, Judge Clemens spoke brightly. "Those Tennessee lands of ours . . . You remember what I've always told you about them. We must never let them go, and one day they'll make us rich. Perhaps if I had stayed in Tennessee, by now we would be worth thousands of dollars."

As his father spoke Sam turned away. When he saw his mother crying in the hall, he realized that Judge Clemens was not going to get well. After dark on March 24, the judge sent for Pamela, his favorite child, kissed her, and murmured, "Let me die." Soon afterward his breath stopped, and Mrs. Clemens hugged Sam to her.

Suddenly the boy thought of the many things he had done to worry his father, of his disobedience and his acts of mischief. He went into another room to weep and there Mrs. Clemens found him. She brought him back into the room in which the judge lay, his face serene and rested.

"Ma," Sam began, "I know I've sometimes been bad, and—"

"That's all over," his mother told him. "You must promise you'll be a better boy, promise that you won't break my heart."

He promised, and asked, "Will I have to keep on going to school? Can't I do something to help? Anything . . ."

"We'll see," Mrs. Clemens answered, and it was understood that before too long they would try to locate work for him.

That night Mrs. Clemens and Pamela woke to see a small figure in white slowly entering their room.

"Sam, Sam!" His mother led the sleepwalker back to bed. But for several nights the disturbed boy wandered about the rooms.

Meanwhile Orion returned to St. Louis to work harder than ever as a printer to help the family. Pamela started giving piano lessons to children, and before long she went to another town to conduct classes. But times continued to be hard for the family, and they moved twice more.

Even in these trying days, Sam derived amusement from an episode that grew out of their several changes of residence. Orion, an absent-minded young man, arrived from St. Louis one night, planning to surprise them. Leaving the steamboat after midnight, Orion walked to the house in which he had last seen them, tiptoed up the back steps to the dark room he had occupied, and got under the covers.

Someone was already there. Thinking it must be his brother, Orion snuggled up. The other figure reached over, felt his whiskers and cried out in a high feminine voice: "It's a man!" Orion had slipped into the room and the bed of a spinster who now lived there with her family.

Leaping up, he threw on his clothes while the woman screamed. As he raced down the stairs he bumped into the woman's brother, who had a butcher knife in his hand. Only when Orion called out did the man recognize him.

After explanations were made, the new occupants suggested that the next time Orion wished to surprise his family, he first make sure where they lived.

The same year, an incident occurred that made Sam Clemens think a great deal. It involved the family of Tom Blankenship and a slave. Tom had an older brother, Bence, who lounged around town and did a few odd jobs. Nobody expected much of Bence.

One day rumors spread that a slave had managed to escape from his owner and row or swim across the Mississippi to the swampy Illinois side. The owner advertised for weeks that he would give fifty dollars for the runaway's return. But no one knew his whereabouts.

One morning Sam noticed Bence Blankenship rowing across the river far more energetically than usual, with a package in his boat. Several days later the same thing happened, and Tom Blankenship accidentally dropped a hint of what his brother was doing. Little by little Sam learned what was going on. Bence had found the slave hiding in a swamp, and the frightened man had begged him: "Please, don't give me up. Just let me stay here."

Sam knew that the fifty-dollar reward would have meant a great deal to Bence, and the youth must have been very much tempted. But Bence felt sympathy for the runaway slave, and, in any case, he did not like slaveholding. So he brought food to the man and caught fish to help keep him alive.

Sam said nothing to anybody about the situation. The story reached unfriendly ears, however, and several woodcutters decided to track down the slave and get the reward.

The runaway saw them coming and tried to escape. Working his way through the swamp, he remained safe until he reached Bird Slough, an especially treacherous waste. Fighting his way forward, he slipped under the surface and disappeared.

Hearing the tale, Sam was very sad. But afterward he held a higher opinion of Bence Blankenship, a poor man who had passed up a chance to get a large sum of money in order to protect another human being. In later years Sam was to make the runaway slave and the situation immortal in American literature.

10

Printer's Devil

For Sam, carefree days were suddenly over. At twelve he was neither a boy nor a man, but his mother needed his help to keep the family going. When his brother Orion tried to sell the Tennessee lands on which Judge Clemens had placed his highest hopes, he could find no buyers. Yet the Clemenses needed money badly. One day Sam picked up a newspaper and handed it to Mrs. Clemens. "Ma," he said, "the *Gazette*'s looking for a helper."

Jane Clemens went to the newspaper office with Sam. The editor was not greatly impressed when he saw the boy. Sam seemed small, and the job would require a lot of labor, the man explained. "Let me try," Sam appealed, and the editor finally agreed. He explained that later he might teach young Clemens a little printing, but to start with, Sam would do odd jobs, go on errands, and deliver the *Gazette*.

"Deliver it? Gee, I'll like that," Sam replied. He would be going to new places, seeing new sights. So he began, working part of each day and continuing in school for a time. As a paper boy he became "an object of interest to every dog in town. If I had saved up all the bites I ever received, I could have kept Dr. Pasteur busy for a year."

Pausing at various houses, Sam would talk about the day's happenings. In Hannibal, as elsewhere along the Mississippi, a major part of the news was provided by the river. "New steamboat's coming," he would announce. Or: "They say river traffic's bigger than ever in St. Louis and New Orleans." All too often, he told of grim explosions on the river. "Forty people killed. Boilers exploded, and the boat burned right down."

Within six months Sam had a second employer, Mr. Ament of the *Courier*, who was drawn to Hannibal in 1848 by the increasing river trade. From neither publisher did the boy receive pay; instead he had board and lodging.

While Sam was learning his trade as a printer, Mr. Ament agreed to provide him with two suits of clothes a year. One suit Sam never saw; the other turned out to be a set of Mr. Ament's old clothes. The man, alas, was twice Sam's length and width. Enveloped by the garments, Sam felt as if he were moving inside a circus tent. He had to turn the trousers up to his ears, he said, to make them short enough.

One of his fellow apprentices was an easygoing giant named Wales McCormick. Sam said later that Wales "had no principles and was delightful company." Enormous though he was, Wales also had to take a suit of Mr. Ament's old clothes. It was as small on him as Sam's was large, clinging to Wales like a banana skin.

As for food, the Ament family provided so little for Sam and the two other apprentices that they were often hungry. At times Sam slipped away to his mother's quarters and ate the leftovers there.

Eventually Sam and Wales hit on a way to keep themselves from going hungry. Most of the paper's subscribers didn't pay in money; they brought the publisher sacks of onions, wood, sugar, pumpkins, watermelons, and other produce. These supplies were stored in the cellar of the Ament house. Before long Sam and Wales were creeping to the cellar to "borrow" onions and potatoes and smuggle them to the print shop, where they cooked them on a small stove near the pallets on which they slept. Sam was learning many new skills.

As a cub, or "printer's devil," the boy came to love the dusty printing office, with its smell of ink and rolls of paper. Every day he rose early, built the fire, went to the pump for water, and gathered broken metal type left on the floor. Then he swept up the office and sorted the good type. He also washed the rollers and newspaper "forms" and moistened the paper so that it would "take" the ink.

Afterward, when others had set the columns of type in place, Sam turned the handles of the printing press and watched a sheet go in one side and out the other. He had to make certain there was just enough ink. If there was too little the words would come out a grayish color, but if there was too much the ink would come off on the reader's hands.

Soon Sam received what he had been yearning for— permission to set type. Being small, he had to stand on a box to reach the cases in which the various letters were kept. Holding a composing stick, he formed words and sentences, line by line. At first he worked slowly, but before long he was going at a much faster rate.

When the paper suddenly needed matter to fill a column, Sam helped Mr. Ament find something to copy from another journal, or occasionally made up a few lines of his own. Although he had read as little as possible in school, he now scanned dozens of newspapers from New Orleans, Memphis, New York, and other great cities. A printing office, he said later, was an educational institution. As he set stories into type, he learned about national events, affairs in Europe and Asia, poetry, essays, the art of satire.

More and more frequently Sam darted up the street with "special news." The subject was war, the war of the United States against its smaller neighbor, Mexico. Almost any tidings from the front met with quickened interest. Sam, Tom, and the others in their gang gathered at the dock to see groups of young men ride off by steamboat to join the fighting. One of Sam's former fellow-students, an "elderly pupil" as he called him, went off to war. The younger boys considered it unfair that they could not go too. "We'll be with them soon," Sam assured his friends. They were not, however. The hostilities ended before they were old enough to participate, and Sam was very disappointed.

Work or no work, Sam still saw Tom Blankenship, John Briggs, and other cronies. He made certain he was at the river landing with them when Hannibal received its first minstrel show. It was a glittering event. Sam sat spellbound through the evening of songs, jokes, and "cakewalks"—those astonishing dances with their long steps and strutting movements. From then on, Sam saw every minstrel show that came to town.

Something even more exhilarating also arrived by river—a theater on a steamboat, or a "showboat" as people called it. For weeks the paper proclaimed its arrival and hours before the vessel rolled in, curious boys lined the landing. There, in awed silence, they watched the glorious stage figures promenading the deck, a certain glamour setting them off from every-body else.

Later Sam stared up at the beautiful leading lady and her "aged" father—who was frequently younger than she was, but wore a powdered wig. He hated the villain with his greased handlebar mustache, and admired the handsome hero who suffered every pain for the lovely girl and received his reward at the last curtain. Between the acts everybody in the drama stepped out to sing and dance. Whatever they did, Sam considered it magnificent.

Circuses also came to Hannibal—big and small, good and not so good, and a few outright fakes. They seldom had as many elephants as they claimed—and sometimes no elephant at all; and often the "wild beasts" had an extremely tame air. But Sam happily absorbed the whole spectacle, and so did Mrs. Clemens. She liked shows as much as her son did.

For nearly two years the members of the Clemens family had been separated. But now that Sam's apprenticeship to Mr. Ament was about to end, his mother wondered if they couldn't be together again. She did not like the thought of Orion living in St. Louis, Pamela teaching in another town, and Sam under a third roof. Then, overnight, an opportunity for a reunion developed.

For a long time Orion had hoped to operate a paper in Hannibal. After some delay he came home, borrowed several hundred dollars, and in September 1850, started his own journal, the *Western Union.* Pamela returned, Henry became a cub printer like Sam before him, and Orion made an offer to Sam. He would pay his brother $3.50 a week as a printer and editorial assistant. Sam hesitated. He knew that Orion had financial problems and might not be able to spare even that small amount. Still, it would be good to rejoin the family, and he accepted. He never received a cent of pay, Sam said later, but at least he was free of the miserly Aments.

Orion had always been impractical, and also of a highly changeable disposition. Before long he bought out a rival and published the combined newspapers under the title the *Hannibal Journal.* At the same time he lowered advertising and subscription rates. As a business venture, the paper's future did not look promising.

But everybody worked hard, and Mrs. Clemens

tried to provide the best meals she could with the little money they had. Sam recalled that they lived on a steady diet of bacon, butter, bread, and coffee.

A new apprentice arrived from a country village to board with the family—the tall, gentle Jim Wolfe.

Jim was one of the shyest people Sam had ever met; he could barely speak in the presence of a girl. At once Sam started to play endless jokes on him.

One winter night Pamela gave a candy pull. Sam and Jim were considered too young for Pamela's friends, and were happy to avoid the party. They went upstairs to bed, and for an hour or so Sam listened to the voices of the couples below. Then he heard the beginning of a fight between a pair of cats near the chimney of a first-floor roof.

Unable to sleep, the boy went to Jim's room and found the apprentice sitting up in his nightshirt, furious about the cats. "Why don't you go out and drive them away?" Sam asked with a mischievous look.

"For two cents I would," Jim snapped.

"Of course you would," Sam replied. "Who doubts it?"

"Maybe you doubt it." Jim was rising to the bait, like a fish to a tempting worm.

"Oh, no," said Sam with a superior grin. "You're always doing wonderful things—you *say*."

This remark settled the matter; Jim was going after the cats. The chimney stood only a short way from the window, but six inches of ice-covered snow lay upon the peaked roof. As Sam watched Jim lower himself from the window, he saw that Pamela and her guests were in the vine-covered arbor below, waiting for the pans of warm candy to cool on the snowy ground.

Jim dropped to his hands and knees and felt his way along the narrow rooftop toward the cats. Years later Sam would laugh as he remembered the scene: Jim slipping every few inches, the cats waving their tails and snarling, and the couples talking below, unaware of what was happening. Each time Jim appeared about to roll off, Sam's hopes rose. But the apprentice just managed to cling on.

At last Jim reached the chimney. Putting out his hand, he missed the cats—and lost his balance. He cascaded down the ice-coated roof, his feet flying, his thin nightshirt flapping.

Crashing through the arbor vines, Jim landed among the saucers of warm candy. As Sam put it, even with his clothes on, the youth could not face a girl. But now, in his nightshirt, Jim was in agony. The young ladies screamed and covered their eyes. Jim picked himself up, dripping taffy and kicking aside broken dishes, and fled upstairs.

Sam repeated the story everywhere. Jimmy McDaniel, the boy with the poor teeth, roared so loudly that Sam thought he would laugh the teeth right out of his mouth. This was one of the first times Sam had ever told a humorous tale, and the enjoyment of his audience delighted him. Some years later, putting the incident on paper, he amused thousands of other people with it.

Before long Sam was having fun in print. Orion usually produced a dull newspaper, consisting primarily of long, gushy poems and poor fiction. It printed little news about Hannibal itself. Sam attempted to add some life to the paper by joking about happenings around them. Once he described a young lady walking along the river wearing the daring, newfangled style of bloomers. A Mississippi pilot became so excited at the sight, Sam claimed, that he started to steer his boat up the hill!

Jim Wolfe gave Sam material without knowing it. Once a fire broke out near the printing office, and Sam told how Jim performed a "noble deed" of rescue. He grabbed a broom, a mallet, a wash pan, and a dirty towel, and rushed forth to place this valuable collection in a safe place—ten blocks away. Then the hero raced breathlessly back, to find that the fire was all out.

Soon afterward Sam sent a story to a Boston humor magazine, the *Carpet-Bag*. It was published in May of 1852—the first anecdote ever to come out with the name or initials of Samuel Clemens. Appropriately its setting was the Mississippi, but of an earlier day.

As a brightly painted steamboat stopped for fuel at Hannibal, a magnificently dressed dandy with a large mustache decided to impress the female passengers.

Gazing down from the deck, the dude made out a husky backwoodsman on the bank. He told the women to watch while he scared the fellow into a fit.

Sticking his bowie knife into his belt, he pulled out a pair of horse pistols and approached the woodsman, shouting: "So I've found you at last! You're the man I've been hunting for weeks. Well, say your prayers." He thrust both pistols at the river man. "You'll make a fine barn door, and I'm going to drill the keyhole through you."

But the simple fellow did not react as expected. Looking the city slicker up and down, he slowly drew back, made a fist, and pounded it between the stranger's eyes. A moment later the amazed dandy found himself sitting in the low water, blinking and asking what had happened to him. As he felt his way back to the boat, the woodsman had a final word: "I say, you, next time you come around drillin' keyholes, don't forget yer old acquaintances!"

When Orion occasionally had to leave town, Sam took over the newspaper. He wrote articles under the ridiculous name of "W. Epaminondas Adrastus Blab." He made fun of silly poetry addressed to young women and needled the editors of rival newspapers.

Infuriated people often called at the paper to thrash the man responsible for a story. On discovering that the boyish acting-editor had written it, they left. When Orion returned, he usually managed to pacify the injured parties. Despite his caution, he did not prevent Sam from writing accounts like this one:

TERRIBLE ACCIDENT

500 MEN KILLED AND MISSING!!!

We had set the above head up, expecting (of course) to use it, but as the accident hasn't happened, yet, we'll say

(To be continued.)

The family had ups and downs. Pamela married Will Moffett, an old friend of the family, and went to live in St. Louis. A cow ambled into the printing office, knocked over a type case, and chewed up valuable rollers. After that two fires further damaged the paper.

Sam had spent about two years with his brother's

newspaper. Now nearly eighteen, he was growing tired of hard work without pay. He began to wonder if he might not find opportunity elsewhere, perhaps in another town on the Mississippi. An unpleasant incident settled his future. Hearing of a bargain in a secondhand gun, he went to Orion to ask if he could have a few dollars to buy it. Orion shouted his reply: "That would be plain extravagance. What are you thinking about?"

Sam felt deeply hurt. Nodding quietly, he went to Mrs. Clemens and said, "Ma, there's no place for me here. I'm going to try St. Louis."

Protests came to his mother's lips, but she stopped them. She yearned to have him stay with her, yet perhaps his future did lie elsewhere. She drew out her Bible: "I want you to take hold of the other end, Sam, and repeat these words: 'I do solemnly swear that I will not throw a card or drink a drop of liquor while I'm gone.'"

Then Mrs. Clemens kissed him. He said good-bye to Tom Blankenship, Will Bowen, and Laura Hawkins, and finally to his brother Henry. He would miss them a great deal, and he knew it. One evening in May he boarded the night boat which was to take him down the Mississippi.

Ordinarily Sam would have been overjoyed to step aboard a steamboat. But tonight he felt sad. Unable to sleep, he walked about the decks.

As he studied the engines and watched the pilot-house from below, his old interest returned. How much he wanted a steamboat job right now! But Sam knew only one way to make a living—in the printing trade. For the present he had to stick to that. He returned to his cabin and finally, listening to the pound of the paddle wheels, dozed off.

11

Wanderer

The waterfront at St. Louis was the busiest, most exciting place Sam had ever seen. He leaned against a post, taking in the river people, the river cargoes, the river smells. Hundreds of wagons and hills of freight occupied every inch of space, and steamboats lined the docks for almost a mile.

"Watch out, boy!"

"Take care down there!"

Sam dodged drays and jumped out of the path of fast-moving wagons as he inspected one vessel after another, identifying each by the insignia that hung between the double smokestacks. He watched the rush of people when departure time approached; he thrilled to the ringing of bells, the cries of steamboat mates, the calls of roustabouts: "Leavin' right now . . . Everybody step lively!"

Sam sighed. Some day he might be riding the steamboats, as he yearned to do. For the present he had to get back to his office.

Sam was staying with his sister, Pamela, in St. Louis and working as a newspaper printer. It was good enough employment, yet his mind was on other things. He felt more restless than at any other time in his life.

After a couple of months he heard of the great Crystal Palace Exhibition (1853) in New York, a kind of World's Fair of the day. He told himself he *had* to see the shimmering displays of jewelry, tapestries, and thousands of other rich goods under the gigantic dome. Taking his small savings, Sam said good-bye to Pamela and her husband and took his first ride on a railroad train. It was an interesting enough experience, but when he arrived in New York, exhausted and coated with dust and cinders, he decided that he much preferred the wind-swept glory of a steamboat.

For days Sam walked about the big city, gawking at everything, marveling at the size of it all. When his money was gone, he located a printing job. After a time his pay increased, and he received a full four dollars a week. He saved his funds and sent part of them to his mother.

Soon St. Louis called him back. Again he worked as a printer and walked up and down the levee, watching the ever-changing procession of the steamboats. To St. Louis came new word of the family. Orion had married and set up another printing office at Keokuk, Iowa, another Mississippi River town. Mrs. Clemens and young Henry had joined Orion. Couldn't Sam be with them again? Orion promised to pay better than before.

After some hesitation Sam agreed, and in the winter of 1854 he went to work again for his older brother. The only trouble was that he still received no salary. Then Orion took him into partnership, giving him the impressive title of part-proprietor. But things did not improve. Now he was not entitled to any pay at all!

A letter from Hannibal added to his discomfort. His friend Will Bowen had become a cub pilot, learning the river under the direction of a regular master. And Will's brother was also on the Mississippi. Sam's old ambition to be a pilot stirred again. But, asking questions, he discovered that simply to study under a regular pilot cost several hundred dollars. He could only wait until something happened in his favor.

For Sam Clemens it was a time of drifting until he found a new direction to follow. In these months Sam read far more than before, making up for many of the things he had missed as a mischievous boy in school. He absorbed history, geography, and English literature, and developed a lively concern with happenings of the world.

He also cultivated what was to become a lifetime habit of reading in bed. One night he became fascinated with a volume that reported the adventures of an American navy lieutenant who had explored the fabulous Amazon River, far away in South America.

Tigers, crocodiles, and other wild beasts, breathtaking scenery, wonderful risks and dangers—Sam read and reread every word. From then on, Sam had "Amazon fever" in his blood.

One cold November day in 1856, the wind carried a scrap of paper past him. As it landed against the edge of a building, Sam reached out and gathered in a fifty-dollar bill. He had never seen so much money. This must be fate, helping him on his way.

For several days Sam advertised in the newspaper to learn if anybody had lost the bill. Nobody came forward, and he took that as another good omen. He was twenty-one now and it was time to move on, time to start the journey that would take him to the distant reaches of another continent.

Sam had to accumulate more funds for his trip to South America. Leaving Orion's employment for the last time, he went to Cincinnati and labored steadily for several months. With the coming of spring 1857, he made his plans; he was going to ride down the river to New Orleans and embark there for the far-off Amazon.

As he climbed aboard the small steamboat *Paul Jones*, Sam was sharply aware of his old love for the Mississippi. He heard the clanging of the bell, the shrill blowing of the whistle; he saw the lifting of the gangplank. He was on his way. For days he went about the vessel, watching everything, listening to everything. He was a *traveler*. . . . He rolled the word in his mouth and, as he said later in his humorous way, nothing had ever tasted so fine.

Resting casually against a railing, Sam looked down with something close to pity when the steamboat passed a plain little town or woodyard. How those people must envy him. He sneezed to draw attention. When several of them glanced up, he yawned carefully and tried to seem bored.

Sam longed to talk with the members of the crew, but they were all too busy. For a day or so he marveled at the big, loud-mouthed mate. The mate never asked someone to lift a plank; instead he yelled: "Here, now, start that plank forward! *What're* you about? Snatch it, snatch it! . . . There, there, I tell you, snatch it!"

One day he heard the mate call for somebody to bring him a capstan bar, a lever to operate part of the equipment. Sam jumped eagerly forward. "Tell me where it is, and I'll fetch it." Later he said that if a ragpicker had volunteered to perform a delicate diplomatic mission for the emperor of Russia, the man could not have been more astonished at his impudence. The mate stared at him for a long time, then growled: "Well, if this don't beat the devil!" With that he ignored Sam altogether.

His spirits shattered, Sam sought the humblest crew member on the boat, an elderly night watchman. At first the watchman paid scant attention to him. But Sam gave him a new pipe, and before long he was sitting beside the old man by the great bell on the steamboat's hurricane deck. The watchman began to talk and Sam was impressed to find that he was the son of an English earl. When his father died, a cruel mother had turned him out.

Sam drank in his words eagerly as the watchman went on with tales of a career full of bloodshed, narrow escapes, and wild adventures. For several days the old man held him spellbound. It was not till later that Sam found out that none of the tale was true.

From the start of the trip Sam had had his eye on the most glittering figure of all, the *Paul Jones* pilot. Day after day he studied Mr. Horace Bixby, a neat, dapper man with an air of quiet, unquestioned authority. Although Sam knew that few pilots liked to have an outsider in the pilothouse, he thought that perhaps, if he chanced upon Mr. Bixby in a good humor, he might talk to him about the river. He might even ask if he could someday be a pilot.

Sam decided to take the risk. That morning Mr. Bixby happened to have a sore foot, which had an important effect on what followed. As the pilot stood at the wheel, a voice behind him said, "Good morning."

Mr. Bixby answered without glancing around. "Good morning."

A silence followed, and Sam's voice came nearer. "How would you like a young man to learn the river?"

This time Mr. Bixby looked back. "I wouldn't. Cub pilots are more trouble than they're worth."

It wasn't a promising beginning, but Sam went on: "I'm a printer, and I don't like it. Thought I might go to the Amazon."

Mr. Bixby showed a slight flicker of interest. "What makes you pull your words that way?" he asked, referring to Sam's drawling speech.

"You'll have to ask my mother," Sam replied. "She pulls hers, too."

The pilot laughed, but said nothing more.

Sam started again: "Do you know the Bowen boys?"

"Very well. Will's a good one. Did his first steering for me." The pilot was beginning to thaw out.

"Come over beside me. What's your name?"

Sam told him and the two stood together, watching the water ahead of the boat. Then Mr. Bixby asked, "Do you drink? Gamble?"

Twice Sam said no. The pilot persisted. "Do you swear?"

"Not for amusement," Sam told him. "Only when I'm under pressure."

The reply made Mr. Bixby smile, and he asked: "You ever do any steering?"

Sam remembered the many boats in which he had enjoyed himself. "I've steered everything on the river except a steamboat."

"Very well." To Sam's complete astonishment, the pilot turned and said: "Take the wheel and see what you can do with a steamboat."

Clearly Mr. Bixby liked Sam. Also, because of his sore foot, he wanted a chance to rest on the bench. Nervously the boy jumped forward. The pilot sat right behind him, of course, and from time to time he called directions to Sam. Nevertheless, Sam felt a swift thrill of excitement, and perspiration formed on his palms. Was he going to make a blunder that would ruin his chances?

Apparently he did nothing of the sort. After a while Mr. Bixby spoke as if he had made up his mind that Sam might do for a cub. "The only way I'd take on someone for the river," said Mr. Bixby, "would be for money. Five hundred dollars." For this a "learner" slept and ate free while he was on the vessel, but he had living expenses on land.

The five-hundred-dollar figure made Sam swallow hard. "I've got a lot of Tennessee land, and I'd give you two thousand acres."

"No." The pilot was emphatic. "I already have too much of that kind of property."

Sam reflected. Perhaps he could borrow a hundred dollars from Pamela's husband. "I could give you a hundred and pay the rest when I earned it on the river."

Mr. Bixby seemed to find this agreeable, but a decision was postponed. For the rest of the trip Sam stayed mainly in the pilothouse, and he found himself thinking less and less about South America. When he reached New Orleans, he asked how soon a ship would leave for the far-off Amazon River. "Why, there's no such ship going from here," a clerk informed him, "and probably won't be in this century."

Suddenly Sam felt relieved. So much for the Amazon. He raced over to see Mr. Bixby, and they completed their agreement. The next day he would begin in earnest, launching into that exciting part of his life, which he would remember for the rest of his days.

That night Sam stared with his mouth wide open at

the teeming waterfront of New Orleans, the liveliest city he had yet seen. He went along the odd, part French, part Spanish streets, with their iron balconies, colorful archways, and fountains sending up jets of water in the dim evening. He put his head into rollicking cafés and fine restaurants where he saw plates piled high with shrimp, crabs, oysters, and dozens of other delicacies he could not name. He saw women in elaborate hats, men in stiff suits and tall collars, entertainers, and street urchins. And he remembered what someone had once told him: "Anything on earth you want to see, you'll find it in New Orleans."

12

Cub Pilot

The next day, elbowing his way through the crowd near the wharves, Sam felt suddenly important. If these people only realized that he was a future pilot. With an air of great dignity he strode up to the pilothouse. The *Paul Jones* was leaving again for St. Louis at four P.M., the usual starting time for steamboats, and he would be there with Mr. Bixby until their watch ended at eight.

The engines throbbed; smoke billowed from the funnels. The pilot's hands tightened on the wheel and the *Paul Jones* rolled away from shore. Mr. Bixby headed upstream past the many other boats anchored along the levees, those mounds of earth that kept the giant river from overflowing. And then, just as if he were giving Sam the most unimportant of instructions, Mr. Bixby said: "Take her over."

Catching at the wheel, Sam felt his heart miss several beats. They were moving so close to the other vessels that they almost scraped the paint off them. Breathing hard, he pulled toward the middle of the river. There, that was much better.

"What are you up to, you fool?" The pilot snatched the wheel back and returned the boat to what looked like a disastrously narrow path beside the other vessels. Swallowing hard, Sam watched in uneasy silence. After a time the angry flush left the back of the pilot's neck, and he explained.

Going upstream a pilot always "hugged the bank," because the water there was calm. Only when he went down the river did he stay in the center, where the powerful current pushed him swiftly on his way. Sam let out a deep sigh and decided privately that he would like to be only a downriver pilot, and let others go upstream.

As they rode on Mr. Bixby called to him: "That's Six-mile Point." "Here comes Nine-mile Point." Although every such spot looked alike to Sam, he nodded politely. Several times the pilot gave the wheel to him, and Sam found himself making one miscalculation after another.

Going too close to land, he almost chopped away

the edge of a Louisiana sugar plantation. Then, to make up for the error, he ventured much too far from shore. With each error he received a sharp reprimand.

At eight P.M., the exhausted Sam saw the watch end. After supper he went to bed and slept heavily. He woke up to find a lantern being flashed in his face, and a night watchman shaking him. "Turn out, turn out!" the man rumbled at him.

Sam yawned. What did the fellow want? Not bothering to find out, he rolled over and dozed off. Soon the watchman reappeared and Sam, awakened again, snapped at him: "Why are you bothering me in the middle of the night? Now I won't get back to sleep again." With that, he pulled the covers over his head.

A few minutes later Mr. Bixby stood beside his bunk, scowling down at him. "Time for your next watch! Get up and get up fast, if you know what's good for you." In a few seconds Sam was walking into the pilothouse with Mr. Bixby, wearing some of his clothes and carrying the rest under his arm.

This rude awakening came as a shock to Sam, who had never considered going to work in the middle of the night. "I knew that boats ran all night," he said later, "but somehow I had never happened to reflect that somebody had to get up out of a warm bed to run them."

In the dark, they seemed to be riding on a gray lake with only a vague shore on either side. One of the officers approached Mr. Bixby to say, "Sir, we have to land at Jones's plantation."

"Upper end, or lower?" Mr. Bixby inquired.

"Upper."

"Can't do it," Mr. Bixby answered. "The tree stumps are standing out of the water at this stage of the river. It'll have to be the lower end."

Sam asked himself if Mr. Bixby really thought he could pick out any plantation at all, much less a certain part of it, on such a night. To Sam's astonishment Mr. Bixby proceeded to do just that. The pilot pulled a signal rope, a bell sounded, and Mr. Bixby murmured: "Jones's plantation, lower end."

Sam shook his head in disbelief, but a moment later the vessel nudged the land to allow the sugarcane grower to step ashore. More than ever, Sam wondered at the remarkable capacities of Mr. Bixby.

As they continued up the river the pilot swung around. "What was the first point we passed above New Orleans?"

Sam had a quick reply. "I don't know."

"You don't *know*! Then tell me the second point. You don't know that either? Well, the third."

His face showing his shame, Sam admitted that he recalled none of them. Mr. Bixby spat out his words: "You're the stupidest dunderhead I ever saw, so help me Moses! You don't know enough to pilot a cow down a lane. Why do you suppose I told you those names?"

"Er—to be entertaining, I thought."

Like a bull with a red flag before him, Mr. Bixby stormed on and on. He was so furious that he failed to see a small boat beside them, and ran over its steering oar. The crew of the little craft shouted and shook their fists at him.

This made Mr. Bixby still angrier. Sticking his head out, he matched them oath for oath. Sam was suddenly glad that his chief had the opportunity to rid himself of his wrath. Like the Mississippi River in flood time, the pilot was "brimful" of rage, and it had to be released in some fashion.

Finally, his anger spent, Mr. Bixby spoke more kindly to Sam. "My boy, get a memorandum book and whenever I tell you something, put it down. That's the only way. You have to know this river just like A B C."

Sam's heart sank. There were twelve hundred miles of river to be learned. And what about the four-hour watches when he would be off duty and asleep in his cabin? When Sam asked about this, Mr. Bixby answered lightly, "On the next trip, boy, you'll fill in the gaps."

Groaning, Sam set to work. He filled a book with the names of villages and towns, plantations, islands, sand bars, and river bends. Then he sat hunched over the notes, trying to make out what they meant.

After the steamboat reached St. Louis, Mr. Bixby transferred with his new cub to a much bigger vessel, and for the first time Sam learned what real Mississippi splendor could be. He had never known anything like it, on land or water.

Slowly he walked through the sumptuous salon, like an elegant drawing room in a vast mansion. The door of each stateroom was decorated with an oil painting, and chandeliers swayed and glittered from the ceiling. The lower deck seemed as large as a church, and Sam made out what looked like armies of deck hands, firemen, and roustabouts clustered around eight enormous boilers.

The wonder of wonders, though, was the pilot-house, a glass chamber big enough to hold a dance in. He stared at the red and gold curtains, a handsome sofa, a leather-cushioned bench for visiting pilots, a big stove, a showy wheel with inlaid woodwork, a gleaming white cuspidor instead of the usual wooden box with sawdust. And he blinked when a neat waiter in a white apron brought up coffee and tarts and ices.

Now, however, the cub pilot's real troubles started. Riding back to New Orleans he learned that downstream piloting could be even harder than the upstream variety. The current moved so powerfully that the steamboat might be swept too far downward and miss the landing, or might even get out of control. Fighting the strength of the Mississippi, his arm hurt as if a powerful hand gripped it.

Soon Mr. Bixby inquired of him: "What's the shape of Walnut Bend?"

Sam shook his head. "I don't know."

The pilot exploded: "You seem to be more different kinds of a fool than any creature I ever met." Mr. Bixby continued more quietly: "My boy, you've got to have the *shape* of everything in your head. On a very dark night it's the only thing that will save you."

Sam rubbed his chin. "How can I know all that?"

The pilot frowned. "How do you know a hall at home in the dark? You learn the shape of it."

Sam felt helpless. "You mean I have to learn all the thousands of little shifts in the riverbanks, for hundreds of miles, as well as I know the hall at home?"

Mr. Bixby nodded. "Better than that."

Sam gave a deep groan. "I wish I was dead."

"And also . . ." The pilot had worse news. "Even on clear evenings things have different night shapes than day ones. Under starlight, shadows will make you think there's a heavy bank when there's nothing. And, if it's pitch black, you have to drive the boat right into what looks like a solid wall. Only you know it isn't a wall at all. Then, when you're in a gray mist, the bank has no regular shape. And different kinds of moonlight change things, too, and . . ."

Sam clapped his forehead. If he put all that information in his head, it would make him stoop-shouldered! Just then the steamboat's other pilot came on duty and quietly mentioned a point not far ahead of them: "Banks are caving in, and you won't know the old place when we get there."

Sam felt his spirits sink down to the river bottom. So you couldn't depend on the river once you'd learned it. Besides the banks, the sand bars in the Mississippi were constantly altering. One spot became deeper, another more shallow, and the pilot must understand where the shifts were developing with each season of the year!

Sam told himself that a river man must not only learn more than any human being should be allowed to know, but he had to keep on relearning it every day.

From then on he worked in earnest. Going downstream, he would fix his gaze on a certain point, a tree or a hill, and try to "photograph" it in his mind. But before he was able to decide just what it was like, its outline would merge with the general scene. And the same place looked entirely different on the trip upstream.

As Sam tried to absorb all this, the pilot suddenly asked: "Now, how much water did we have in the middle crossing at Hole-in-the-Wall, the trip before last?"

Sam's mouth fell open. "How can I remember *that*?"

Mr. Bixby shook his finger at him. "You've got to remember it—the exact spot and the exact depths the boat was in when we had the lowest water, in every one of the five hundred low places between New Orleans and St. Louis! And you've got to have it all down in your brain, so that you'll never mix the soundings of one trip with another."

Sam faced the pilot in disgust. "When I get so I can do that, I'll be able to raise the dead. Mr. Bixby, I want to retire and be a roustabout. I don't have enough brains to be a pilot. If I had them, I wouldn't have the strength to carry them around, except on crutches."

The pilot shrugged. "You'll do it. When I promise I'll learn a man the river, I'll learn him or kill him." Sam shuddered. Someone, perhaps all of them on this boat, would be killed before *he* mastered the Mississippi.

He never forgot that on him rested the safety of countless human beings and a heavy steamboat worth a quarter of a million dollars or more. The knowledge made him tremble as he slipped through a channel so narrow that the steamboat's stern brushed the branches of overhanging trees, and at the same time avoided the hidden wreck of another craft that might chew his own hull to bits.

Sam was disturbed when another pilot would watch him steer for a while and shake his head. "Clemens, you'll never learn the river." At such times the youth's lips tightened to a thin line.

He would show them.

13

Reading the Water

The next step in Sam Clemens's river education was "water reading." From the beginning he had stood beside old pilots as they frowned down at the river's surface, studying it like the pages of a newspaper. Just what were they looking for? He did not dare ask for fear he would be laughed at. A cub was laughed at often enough as it was.

One day Mr. Bixby inquired: "Do you see that long, slanty line on the water?" When Sam nodded, the pilot explained: "That's the sign of a reef below. Under it there's a solid sand bar, going up and down like the side of a house. Right to the edge of the sand bar there's plenty of water, but mighty little on top. And if you hit it, you can knock the boat's brains out."

Earnestly Sam inclined his head, and Mr. Bixby resumed. "You notice where the line in the water fringes out at the upper end and starts to fade away? That's a low place, the head of the reef. You can just get over it, if you're careful enough. Try it. Cross over now."

Holding his breath, Sam tried to follow the pilot's directions, and Mr. Bixby went on. "She won't want to mount the reef. A boat hates shallow water."

With Sam's hands on the wheel, the vessel did seem at first to fight. But then, while Sam perspired in fear, the steamboat suddenly responded and followed the direction in which he headed it.

"But watch her," the pilot cried. "Watch her like a cat, or she'll get away from you. . . . Let up a little! But keep edging up, little by little, to the spot over there. You see those fine lines on the water? They're signs of little reefs underneath. You must *just miss* the ends of 'em, but run 'em pretty close."

Sam mopped his moist forehead. A moment later Mr. Bixby cried: "Don't crowd *that* place. She's beginning to smell the low water. Look sharp. Ah! Now you've done it!" Sam had "done it" in exactly the wrong way, and Mr. Bixby grew more excited than ever.

"Stop the starboard wheel!" the pilot yelled. "Quick, *set her back*!" Engine bells rang; the boat lurched and rolled toward shore like a frightened animal. Sam and the pilot struggled with the wheel, and eventually the steamboat was under control again.

Considering how difficult the spot had been, the cub had not fared badly. It was a lesson to remember. As he thought it over, Sam studied the water harder than ever.

More and more, as time went on, the river's surface began to resemble the pages of a book. The words were written in a peculiar but clear language, understood only by pilots. It told everything they had to know and, Sam said, it had a new tale to offer every half-hour or so—a tale that never grew dull.

The average person would pay no heed to a certain small ripple. But it warned of possible disaster, for beneath it lay the hulk of a sunken vessel. When he saw a beautiful reddish sunset, Sam reminded himself that there would be a strong wind in the morning. And a floating log meant the river was beginning its springtime rise, and the pilot would have to look around more sharply than ever.

Sam also learned about soundings. When the river was low and a boat approached a particularly shallow spot, it tied up at shore. One of the pilots took a crew of men in a small boat to probe with a pole for the exact depths that lay ahead. The other pilot would keep a close watch by spyglass from the pilothouse.

When the probers had found and marked with a

buoy the shallowest point, they would row out of the path of the steamboat, and the big vessel would work its way through the water. If the leeway was scant, the steamboat would crunch and grind slowly over the sand. The sounding crew waited its chance to scramble back aboard. If they were unlucky and the steamboat caught on the reef, they had to stay on the water until the boat worked its way loose—a process that might take hours.

Sam enjoyed these sounding expeditions. As cub, he was occasionally permitted to shout directions to the rowers: "Starboard, give way! Strong on the larboard!" These were high moments, as he knew the crew and passengers were looking on from the steamboat.

Sam had made friends with another cub pilot named Tom, who was training under the second pilot on the vessel. They got along well until one trip when a pretty girl stepped aboard with her uncle. The man knew both pilots, and the girl spent hours in the pilothouse with Sam and Tom. Each boy told her about his adventures and his many acts of bravery, and a strong jealousy developed between them.

Brooding, Sam watched for a chance to show up his former friend. Suddenly it arrived. About nine thirty one night a decision was made to sound the water around a hard spot that lay ahead. Since Tom's superior was on duty in the pilothouse, Sam's pilot would go out in the small boat, with Sam assisting.

Happily Sam watched the excited passengers line up at the deck rail, the pretty girl among them. The night was black and rainy, the wind blasted about them, and there was more danger than usual. For Sam, this meant a greater chance to show his courage.

As the sounding boat prepared to leave, Sam strode toward it, bundled in his storm outfit. Passing Tom, he muttered sarcastically: "Aren't you glad you don't have to go out tonight?"

Tom growled. "Just for that, you can get the sounding pole yourself. I was going to bring it to you."

Sam blinked in surprise. "The pole's in the sounding boat."

"No, it isn't," Tom replied. "It's been painted and it's up there, drying." Sam raced to get the pole. But just as he ran back, he heard the command from below: "Give way, men."

The sounding boat had left without him. Tom had tricked him and there he was, sitting in Sam's place with the sounding pole next to him. At that moment Sam caught the girl's delighted murmur: "Oh, isn't it terrible for those brave people to have to go out tonight?"

Sam said later that he would rather have been stabbed than miss this great opportunity. In the dark the sounding boat disappeared; he heard the lift and fall of oars, then calls and signals. "They're at the buoy now," someone shouted. Soon they saw a flickering light, and the steamboat churned toward it.

In the pilothouse, Sam felt worse than ever. All at once he heard the pilot's voice. "That's odd. The buoy lantern's out." Nevertheless the big vessel plowed steadily ahead, scraped sand for a few moments and slipped into deeper water. At the same moment there came a cry and a thud. The steamboat's paddle wheel had hit the sounding boat and cut it to bits.

Swiftly the steamboat stopped. Sam ran below, and soon his own chief and most of the others scrambled aboard from the darkness. But two of the men, and also Tom, were nowhere in sight.

Behind him Sam heard the women clicking tongues. "That poor boy . . ." A moment later there rose a weak cry. One of the missing men was making his way toward the steamboat. The voice grew tired. Would the victim drown in the dark? Now they heard the faint call: "I can make it! Stand by with a rope."

In the glow of a torch basket, the chief mate tossed out the rope, and several men pulled the swimmer to safety. It was Tom.

The other two men were never seen again. Tom explained that he had dived under the great paddle wheel of the steamboat, escaping death by inches. He was everybody's hero, and Sam suffered new and worse pangs of jealousy.

"It wasn't so much to dive like that," he protested. "I could have done the same thing." But, alas, nobody paid any attention.

As the leadsmen dropped weighted cords to gauge the river depths, the cry sounded again and again: "*Mark Twain!*" It meant "two fathoms," or twelve feet of water—enough for the steamboat to move safely. For Sam it was a comforting sound.

He had fewer worries now, as even Mr. Bixby gradually came to approve his progress. More than ever Sam realized that of all a pilot's skills his memory was the the most important. It had to be phenomenal. He had to keep in his mind every detail of twelve hundred miles of river, as well as a thousand changes or rumors of changes along the way. He learned to observe scenes unconsciously so that he would note the slightest alteration in the current or the shore.

He would be talking with friends, paying little direct attention to the leadsmen calling monotonously: "Half twain; half twain; half twain." But for a second there might come another message: "Quarter twain." This signified less water, a need for caution. Then the call would be: "Half twain; half twain . . ."

The trained listener would say nothing, but long afterward he would remember just where that minor difference had occurred—the exact point on the riverbank, the location of a nearby bluff, a precise tree. He had "photographed" everything in his mind.

Each year when the snow melted in the north, the river waters began to rise. Sand bars that usually stood out of the water like the top of a warehouse were suddenly covered. Acres of land on either side of the stream were flooded, and an expert pilot could steer through what had formerly been woods and cut twenty-five miles off his course.

But there were different risks. Sometimes the "chutes" through which Sam made his way were so narrow that he could not back out if he saw he had made a mistake. When this happened, he never forgot Mr. Bixby's warning: "You've got to go on, or stay there till next spring!" Happily, he never had to do that.

As a great rise of water moved downriver, it brought with it drifting logs, branches, and sometimes whole trees that had fallen when the shore collapsed. The steamboat had to be steered with special care through this debris. At night the hazard was even worse, especially when an enormous log suddenly showed itself just under the vessel's bow.

Mr. Bixby would snap, "No chance of avoiding that one. We'll have to stop the engine and walk over it." Then Sam would brace himself for the terrible clatter and wild rocking that would continue until the log was free. Now and then the log became stuck, and it had to be worked loose with considerable maneuvering.

High water also brought an endless parade of flatboats, coal barges, scows, and other small craft down the river. Upstream, men filled them with flour, bacon, smoked goods, and other produce and floated them down to market. Steamboat people despised the small boats, and the people of such vessels hated steamboats. The war between them was eternal.

"Look at that thing, right in front of us!" Sam would fume as a barge appeared directly under the steamboat's bow. Sometimes it was hit hard, or simply struck a glancing blow, or an oar would be smashed. By law flatboats were supposed to keep lights showing, but often they went downstream in complete blackness. On evenings described by the steamboat men as "dark as the inside of a cow," the danger of collision doubled.

Now Sam learned another new lesson: A pilot must have full confidence in what he knows. One day Mr.

Bixby remarked that he was going below. "You can handle the next crossing?" he asked.

"I can run it with my eyes shut," Sam replied confidently.

"How much water does it have?"

"I couldn't touch bottom there with a church steeple."

He had been over the spot many times. But to his surprise, Mr. Bixby gave him a long look. "You think so, do you?"

Suddenly Sam's self-confidence was shaken. After Mr. Bixby left, he began to imagine dangers lurking at long-familiar points. In a few minutes he saw what seemed to be signs of low water ahead of him. What should he do?

He seized the bell rope, let it fall, then snatched it up again and pulled it. Turning the vessel in one direction, he spotted dangers there and shifted back. The officers on the lower deck frowned and peered toward the pilothouse. What was wrong?

All of a sudden the men who were sounding the depths called: "Mark four . . . Mark three."

Sam gaped. They were supposed to be in an almost bottomless place, and the water was shoaling up! His hands trembled so that he could not ring. Instead he ran to the speaking tube and shouted to the engineer: "Ben, if you love me, *back her*! Back the immortal soul out of her!"

A second later the door of the pilothouse closed behind him and there was Mr. Bixby, smiling gently. He had been standing behind a smokestack the entire time. With him were several steamboat officers, grinning broadly. Mr. Bixby said, "Sam, didn't you *know* this was deep water?"

"Yes, sir."

"Then you shouldn't have let me or the men doing the sounding, or anybody else, throw you off. And another thing, when you think you're in trouble, don't go into a panic. Keep your head."

Sadly Sam nodded. Would he ever forget this instruction? He never did. For months afterward he heard river pilots chuckling when he passed: "Ben, if you love me, *back her*!"

For a time Mr. Bixby had to serve on another boat, and he transferred Sam to the management of another pilot, on the freighter *John J. Roe*. This was quite a different kind of vessel.

There were few passengers. Most of the officers came from rural sections, and a friendly country flavor prevailed on the boat. In fact, it was a sort of floating farm on the Mississippi. The *John J. Roe* had a piano, and people sat around on the boiler deck at night and enjoyed moonlight dances.

Sam called the *John J. Roe* the slowest boat on the whole planet. When she went downstream, he claimed, she could not even overtake the river's current! For hours he would sit at the piano, singing one of his favorite songs, telling about a horse named Methusalem:

> *Took him down and sold him in Jerusalem,*
> *A long time ago.*

Reluctantly, Sam left the *John J. Roe* for another vessel. One day while his new steamboat was berthed in New Orleans, Sam saw a familiar sight, the *John J. Roe*. Going aboard, he received a loud and hearty welcome from his old friends. It was like going back to his uncle John's farmhouse.

On deck he encountered a new face—a charming fifteen-year-old girl in a white summer dress and plaited pigtails. She was Laura Wright, the daughter of a Missouri judge and a relative of the steamboat pilot. Sam liked her at once and she seemed to return his feelings. For the next few days, he said, he stayed no more than four inches from Laura during all his waking hours. His thoughts were constantly of her. He hoped to meet her again in Missouri or on future river trips, and she appeared pleased when he spoke of the prospect. But suddenly one afternoon someone called out to him: "Your own boat's backing out!"

So intent had he been that Sam had not noticed the other vessel leaving. Racing across the deck of the

John J. Roe, he made a long leap and reached his boat just in time. The ends of his fingers caught on the guard rail, and a crew member dragged him aboard. Then Sam waved a long good-bye to Laura.

Soon afterward he sent her a note. But he never received a reply. Forty years later, after he had become a celebrated man, she wrote to him, and he learned that she had never seen his letter. Had she done so, Sam thought, his life might have been different.

14

Tragedy on the River

It had been months since Sam had seen his brother Henry. He had an idea: Why not get Henry a place on his own vessel?

Sam had just been transferred to the *Pennsylvania*, one of the fastest and most fashionable steamboats in the New Orleans–St. Louis trade. He talked to one of the officers and arrangements were made. Henry could start as a "mud clerk," a poor position but a beginning. Like Sam, he would receive only food and bed while he was on the boat. His job would be to count coal boxes, inspect wood piles when they stopped to load, and do other similar chores. Later, perhaps, the boy might become a full-fledged clerk.

In February 1858, Henry signed on as third clerk of the *Pennsylvania*. Meeting his brother again, Sam felt a burst of affection. Henry looked good, a handsome youth with slightly curling hair and a straightforward manner. He began work with enthusiasm and Sam noticed that others, including the captain, liked Henry. The arrangement was working out well.

For Sam, however, life was suddenly growing difficult. He had been placed on the *Pennsylvania* under a pilot named Brown, and from their first meeting trouble had developed. Sam described Mr. Brown as "a middle-aged, long, slim, bony, smooth-shaven, horse-faced, ignorant, stingy, malicious, snarling, fault-hunting, mote-magnifying tyrant." When Mr. Brown first set eyes on Sam, he yelled: "What's your name?" Sam told him, but Brown never used his name. He preferred to shout *"Here!"* and then give his commands.

"Where were you born?" he asked the cub pilot.

"Florida, Missouri," Sam answered.

Mr. Brown grumbled to himself. "Dern sight better you stayed there."

The man asked several questions about Sam's life and his family, then told him: "Hold up your foot." With a contemptuous look Mr. Brown examined Sam's shoes and frowned. "Well, I'll be derned." The cub pilot never learned what there was to be "derned" about. With that Mr. Brown ignored him completely.

After fifteen long minutes, Brown suddenly

barked, "Here! Are you going to set there all day?"

Leaping forward, Sam apologized. "I've had no orders, sir."

"You've had no *orders*! What a fine bird *we* are. Our father was a gentleman, and *we've* been to school. Orders, is it? I'll learn you to strut around here talking about orders. Get away from the wheel!"

Dazed, Sam moved back, only to hear: "What are you standing there for? Take that ice pitcher down. Move along, and don't be all day about it!" On Sam's return Mr. Brown demanded: "What were you doing down there all that time?" When Sam answered, Brown snapped, "Hmm. Derned likely story."

This was only the beginning. In the following weeks the pilot watched constantly for a chance to roar at the youth. "Worst numskull I ever saw." "Ain't got enough sense to load a stove." "Pull her down! Get away from the wheel." He denounced Sam for steering too close to shore, and for not steering close enough; for "hugging" a bar of sand, and for not hugging it; for firing up without orders, and for waiting for orders.

According to the rules of steamboat life, a cub could not protest against anything that his superior did. But this couldn't keep Sam from imagining violent protests. As he said afterward, he "killed" Brown every night for months—not by the usual, commonplace methods, but in ways that were new and astonishing. One evening, according to Sam, he went to bed in such a fury that he killed Mr. Brown in seventeen different ways!

His brother Henry sympathized with Sam, and so did the captain and the rest of the crew. Yet they could do nothing to help. Sam had to hold his tongue and try to endure.

On one trip, when Sam was in the pilothouse with Brown, Henry ran up with a message for the pilot: "The captain says to stop, sir, at the next landing."

Brown made no response and Sam wondered if he had heard. It was hard to tell because the pilot always ignored underclerks anyway. Later Sam commented that at this point, if he had had two heads, he would have said something to the pilot. But as he had only one, and he did not want it pounded in, he kept still.

The *Pennsylvania* passed up the landing, and within a few minutes the captain walked in and addressed Mr. Brown. "Let the boat come around, sir," he said. "Didn't Henry tell you I wanted to land there?"

"*No*, sir."

"I sent him up to do it," the captain said.

"He did come up, but the derned fool never said anything." Mr. Brown scowled furiously.

The captain faced Sam: "Did you hear Henry?"

Although he hoped to avoid further entanglement

with the pilot, Sam had to stand up for Henry. He answered, "Yes, sir."

Brown turned the color of a turkey's comb. "Shut your mouth. You never heard anything of the sort."

An hour later the innocent Henry reappeared in the pilothouse. Brown roared at him, calling him a liar. Sam's temper rose, and he said: "You lie yourself. He did tell you."

Brown glared from one boy to the other. "You leave the pilothouse," he shouted at Henry. "Out with you!"

As Henry started to go Brown seized a large lump of coal and started after him. A sudden fury ran through Sam. Here was a strong man threatening a young, slight boy, and Sam's brother.

Grabbing a stool, Sam knocked Brown down. In a moment he and the pilot were rolling on the floor, punching each other and shouting. As they struggled, the vessel churned on without a pilot. Luckily the water was high and they were well away from shore.

Brown finally managed to jump up, lifting his spyglass as a weapon, and told Sam: "Now *you* git out." Coolly Sam approached the door, but in a moment all his accumulated grievances came to the surface, and he snapped: "The word is '*get*,' not 'git.' Most people say 'you *were*,' not 'you was.' And whatever you may know, it's not English grammar!"

The noise of the dispute had drawn a crowd below, and when he descended to the deck Sam found the captain among them. Now he was in real trouble, he told himself. Perhaps he could slip over to some corner of the boat and leave at the first chance. But just then the captain approached him with a somber expression. "Follow me," he said.

When they were alone in his cabin, the captain asked a series of questions: Had Sam been fighting with Brown? Did he understand how serious this was—that the ship had been in danger? Had he knocked Brown down?

To each inquiry Sam answered yes. Finally the captain asked, "Did you pound him hard?"

"You might call it that," Sam replied sadly.

The captain let out a deep breath. "I'm glad of it! You've been guilty of a great crime, and don't ever do it again—on this boat, anyway. But lay for Brown ashore, and give him a hard thrashing. I'll pay the expenses. Not a word of this to anyone, boy. And now, out with you, you whelp!"

In a happy daze Sam left, and as he did he heard the captain laugh and slap his side. A little later, however, Brown called on the captain and insisted that Sam Clemens be set ashore when they ended the trip in New Orleans. "I won't turn a wheel on your boat while he stays on," he fumed. "One of us will have to go."

By this time the captain himself was enraged. "Very well. Let it be you." The matter rested there and for the rest of the trip, Sam said, he felt like a freed slave. He spent happy hours playing chess with the other pilot, George Ealer, and listening to him quote the poetry of Shakespeare.

In New Orleans the *Pennsylvania* tied up for three days and the captain tried to find another pilot, but without success. So he was forced to keep Brown until the *Pennsylvania* reached St. Louis. A passage was secured for Sam on the *A. T. Lacey,* which would follow a few days later. At St. Louis, Brown would leave the *Pennsylvania,* and Sam would go back as the cub.

To earn a little money, Sam had been serving occasionally as a night watchman on the New Orleans wharves. He found it a strange experience—"not a sound, not a living creature astir." But he had put the hours to use. "I used to imagine all sorts of situations and possibilities," he said, and often he scribbled them down: bits of stories on which he was to draw in later writings.

On Henry's last evening in New Orleans, he went to the wharves to keep Sam company. They talked of many matters: the family, steamboats, and, after a time, river explosions. There had been several recent tragedies and Sam, as an older river man, began to give his brother advice. "If any accident happens, don't lose your head; the passengers are able to do that. Get to the upper deck and help women and children into the boats. Give every bit of help you can." Impressed, Henry nodded.

The next day Sam saw Henry off. The brothers called good-byes. "See you in St. Louis in a few days," Sam shouted. Two afternoons later he started upstream on the *A. T. Lacey*.

When the boat stopped at Greenville, Mississippi, Sam and some others went ashore. As they reached the dock, a man cried out to them. "Did you hear the news? The *Pennsylvania*'s blown up at Ship Island with a hundred and fifty dead."

All the *A. T. Lacey*'s crew were stunned. For Sam the words meant, above all, his brother Henry. They could get no further information, and there were not yet any lists of dead or injured. In agony Sam waited as the *A. T. Lacey* steamed upriver toward the scene of the accident near Memphis.

That night, reaching Napoleon, Arkansas, Sam jumped ashore to buy a late paper just brought in from Memphis. Holding his breath, he ran his finger down the list of names. *"Saved, Clemens, Henry."* He sighed in relief. But could he be certain? Such accounts were often garbled and names confused.

Sam read more about the disaster. The steamboat had been taking wood from a flatboat behind it when four of her eight boilers exploded. The forward part of the vessel had been tossed into the air, chimneys and all. George Ealer, the pilot who loved Shakespeare, had been steering. Thrown high in the air, he had saved himself by covering his face to protect it from scalding steam.

The captain had been getting a shave in the barber's chair. A moment later he and the barber discovered everything gone around them, ripped away to within an inch of the chair. The captain was saved, but the pilot Brown and some of the other officers had been lost.

Scores of people were thrown into the river and died there. Fire broke out, and many others were badly burned or trapped in the terrible wreckage.

At another town Sam seized upon a later newspaper. His eye stopped at Henry's name among those "injured and expected to die." Forcing back his tears, he sat silent for a long time.

When the steamboat finally reached Memphis, Sam was one of the first to leap ashore. Several people directed him to a public hall that had been turned into a hospital. There he found about forty figures stretched out on mattresses in two rows on the floor.

Practically every head had been wrapped in loose raw cotton, and everywhere were the smells of medicine and oil and burned cloth.

"Henry Clemens?" a man echoed, and pointed. There lay his brother, half conscious, his face red and twisted in its bandages. Sam's heart dropped. Could Henry possibly live?

From others he learned what had happened to the boy. The explosion had thrown him into the river, shocked but seemingly unhurt, and he had begun to swim to shore. He had reached a point only a few hundred yards from land when he turned around and made his way back to the vessel to help in rescuing others. Just what had happened next nobody could be certain, but soon Henry lay on the deck with other stricken people.

The injured were taken to the wood boat, which was cut adrift and finally moored near Ship Island. There they remained for the rest of the day, shivering in the cold night, then burning under the relentless sun. Rescued by another steamboat and taken to Memphis, Henry lay unconscious for another twelve hours.

"What are his chances?" Sam asked again and again. He could get no definite reply; it was too early to tell. For six days Sam sat by the boy. For a time he appeared to improve, and on June eighteenth Sam wrote to Orion's wife: "May God bless Memphis, the noblest city on the face of the earth. She has done her duty by these poor afflicted creatures." He ended his note: "Pray for me, and pray for my poor sinless brother."

All about them, men were groaning. In each case, as the end came near, attendants would lift the victim on a stretcher and carry him to a smaller chamber so that the rest of the wounded would not be upset. Now Sam watched Henry weaken. He looked up as two silent men approached his brother with a stretcher between them. Following them, Sam felt his throat tighten. He remained beside the boy until Henry's head lifted, then fell. His brother was dead.

For weeks Sam walked about with all his grief showing in his face. He blamed himself for Henry's death, remembering the advice he had given the boy before the disaster. The shadow hung over him as he went back to the river. The Mississippi, which had brought Sam so much happiness, had now given him one of the great sorrows of his life.

15

Mississippi Pilot

Sam had become a full-fledged pilot, realizing all his dreams of life on the river. Gradually his sorrow over Henry eased enough so that he could enjoy his career as a master of the Mississippi. He had the deep satisfaction of knowing that he was a very good pilot.

He carried the responsibility for the safety of thousands of lives and for property worth millions of dollars. It was challenging work, demanding the utmost of him. Let him relax at the wrong moment, and his boat could swiftly be turned into a mass of twisted wreckage. To this river he must never fail to give his best, and he never did.

Sam was constantly on the move and he loved the wandering river life. He loved the sweep of the Mississippi, the rush and noise of steamboat departure time, the sight of a serene plantation on a starlit evening.

And in these days he could do things to help his family. He sent gifts to his mother, and arranged for her to enjoy exciting trips by steamboat. He made the unlucky Orion's life easier. The people back in Hannibal, who had often whispered that the flighty youth would "never amount to a hill of beans," now claimed they had known from the beginning that he would make something of himself.

Sam had joined a calling whose rank and prestige were, in a way, greater than any other in the United States. As he put it, a pilot of those days was almost the only completely independent human being left on earth. He noted humorously that kings of the modern day had only the authority allowed them by the people. Holders of public office were checked by the will of the voters, and newspaper editors seldom spoke their minds freely. Every man, woman, and child fretted in servitude of one kind or another, said Sam, but not the Mississippi pilot.

When the vessel tied up at shore the captain commanded, but once it got under way the pilot had full, unquestioned control. If the weather—fog, rain, sudden blasts of wind—seemed too dangerous, he could head toward the bank and remain there as long as he wished. In such matters the pilot consulted nobody. Indeed, United States law ordered him *not* to listen to the commands of others, since it was presumed he knew best how to handle the boat. Sam once witnessed an incident in which a boy of eighteen, a qualified pilot notwithstanding his youth, quietly steered a vessel into what looked like disaster while a white-bearded captain watched in terror, powerless to interfere.

Long before, Sam had observed the marked courtesy shown to the pilot by the captain, the rest of the crew, and the passengers. Later, after seeing much of the world, Sam decided that pilots were the only people who did not betray a certain nervousness when they met traveling foreign princes. Wittily he added: "But then, people in one's own grade of life are not usually embarrassing objects!"

At twenty-three, Sam received an income equal to that of the Vice President of the United States. And few vice presidents won the tribute that went to a pilot.

Even deckhands, firemen, and barbers on a great steamboat shared in the glory. Sam once heard of a crew member who annoyed others at a ball in New Orleans. One of the ball officials went to him and demanded: Who was he, anyway? The crew man drew himself up in vast dignity. Who *was* he? Why, he replied, he fired the middle door on the *Aleck*

Scott! That settled matters; from then on everybody gave him the deference he deserved.

Before long Sam had a new reason for pride. He was invited to be pilot on the *City of Memphis,* one of the biggest boats on the Mississippi and, some claimed, the hardest of all to handle. At once he received elaborate bows from men who had previously assured him he would never learn to pilot a vessel. When he entered pilots' headquarters now, he heard: "Why, how *are* you, old fellow?" "When did you get to St. Louis?" and the like. At times he served as pilot partner to his old superior, Mr. Bixby. To be considered in a class with that veteran pleased him most of all.

Like other pilots of the day, Sam dressed to reflect the glory of his profession. He had always liked bright colors, and now he came forth in reds and yellows, with kid gloves, fine shirts, diamond breastpins. As people said, it was the way a man in his position ought to look.

Sam Clemens had achieved a reputation as a safe pilot. In his years on the river Sam never ran a ship into a bad accident, and that was important to a steamboat owner. Sam himself said that luck had a lot to do with it, and he told of an incident that proved his point.

One day he was preparing to "round to," because

a storm was approaching. He picked a likely bank, then decided to hunt a smoother spot a bit farther down the river. Five miles down he made his landing. The winds roared around the steamboat but damaged it only slightly. Soon afterward, passing the same area, Sam glanced at the place he had first chosen. He hardly recognized it. It had been chewed to bits by the storm, the earth in sad upheaval and half the trees in shreds. "We couldn't have lived five minutes in such a tornado," he said.

Others thought that luck was not the explanation. They said that Sam Clemens had developed the capacity that all real pilots must have to "smell" danger and to make decisions so quickly that they come almost by instinct.

To Sam the Mississippi also meant people. In his years as a river man, he claimed he learned more of human character than a man on shore could learn in forty years.

Whenever he came upon a well-drawn character in a book, he took a warm interest because he had met him before—on the river. Great souls and mean little souls, generous people and petty people, innocents and schemers, fools and wise men—Sam knew them all from the Mississippi.

In his river days, as some pilots later recalled, he was always taking notes, always scribbling stories.

The Mississippi inspired Sam to an early composition that became famous among pilots of the day. For years a famous old pilot had been making stiff, important-sounding statements about conditions on the river. "My opinion for the benefit of the citizens of New Orleans," Captain Isaiah Sellers called it. He would tell of times and events far earlier than anyone else remembered—such as when "Missouri was on the Illinois side," before the Mississippi changed its course.

One day Captain Sellers made a new pronouncement, predicting that the water would be so high at New Orleans that it would reach "four feet deep in Canal Street." The captain added: "Mrs. Turner's plantation at the head of Big Black Island is all underwater, and it has not been since 1815." Thinking over these words, Sam wrote a mock statement, signing it "Sergeant Fathom, one of the oldest cub pilots on the river." According to a newspaper note, he was a very safe one because he never ran his boat after "early candlelight."

Sergeant Fathom predicted that at New Orleans the water would be on the St. Charles Hotel's roof by mid-January. Fathom went on to tell of the year 1763 (many years before steamboats were invented), when he claimed he had gone down the river on the old *Jubilee* with a "Chinese Captain and a Choctaw Indian crew." And, to prove his antiquity, Sergeant

Fathom described how "me and De Soto discovered the Mississippi." Hundreds of readers roared, and the account became a classic.

These were great days on the river. It was the most prosperous period of the Cotton Kingdom, when fields of white blanketed the Deep South. On the steamboats rode emigrants from abroad, eastern farmers on their way to fresh lands, evangelists, circus troupes, quiet mechanics, hot-tempered duelists—a cross section of the people of the New World. Below the main deck, roustabouts worked, joked, and danced. And everywhere was the uncertain light of lanterns, the throb of engines, the rush of steam.

These were the days of thrilling races between steamboats, the subject of hundreds of songs and stories. Although Sam himself took no part in these races, he watched every one he could, crying encouragement along with the other thousands of spectators. At New Orleans, Memphis, Baton Rouge, St. Louis, and hundreds of town landings they lined up to watch—speculating, arguing, scanning the water.

Down at the Crescent City, as many called New Orleans, two ships would wait, their officers poised in nervous anticipation. A gun sounded, steam shrieked, and the vessels churned forward, sending black smoke spiraling into the sky.

To the sound of brass bands, the steamboats flew by the shore. Mile after mile they would remain in sight of each other, or separated by only a short distance. Throngs would stand for hours for a look at the racers as they swept by. And in the end, the cheers were deafening as the victors crossed the line, to set another mark in the long record book of the Mississippi.

It was a glowing age, Sam Clemens thought. Its like had never been seen before, in America or anywhere else. He would have liked nothing better than to ride on through the years at the wheel of a steamboat. But, in a way that neither Sam nor anybody else could have guessed, the "glory times" of the Mississippi River were approaching an end.

For generations the South and North had faced each other in growing hostility over slavery and related matters. Early in 1861, the Confederacy formed, and the American union fell apart. For four years a brutal war shut down the river. There were no shipments of cotton and flour, hides and bacon, and no thousands of travelers along the liquid highway.

Like many others, Sam had to find another occupation, and he left the Mississippi. The years ahead were crowded for him: silver mining in Nevada, gold hunting in California, newspaper work in San Francisco, roving days in Europe and the Far Eastern countries, lecturing and eventually fame as the author of books over which people would laugh and cry and shake their heads in admiration.

But no matter where he went, two things would always be in Sam's heart: his town of Hannibal and the broad Mississippi, "shining in the sun." In book after book he wrote of them. In his tales of Huckleberry Finn and Tom Sawyer he pictured the town and his boyhood there, and in his *Life on the Mississippi* he described for people everywhere the stirring pageant of the river as he saw it.

To millions the Mississippi is Mark Twain's river. For his pen name Sam Clemens took "Mark Twain," which, as we have already seen, meant "safe water." For him the two words had a glorious ring. They soon became known to children and adults all over the world.

Through the generations, millions of his readers have asked to see "the places that Mark Twain described to us." They flock to Hannibal to hunt for a house where Sam Clemens once lived, to look at the "Tom Sawyer cave," to stare from the riverbank toward Glasscock's Island, where Sam and his friends used to hunt turtle eggs. Proudly the Missouri town shows to the world statues of the two young men whom Sam made the most famous in America—Huck Finn and Tom Sawyer.

Along the river another boy remains—unseen, but there in spirit. It is Sam Clemens himself, who will never die because, for all his readers, he made the Mississippi live.